Founders, Freelancers & Rebels

Founders, Freelancers & Rebels

How to Thrive as an Independent Creative

Helen Jane Campbell

BEP
BUSINESS EXPERT PRESS
Leader in applied, concise business books

Founders, Freelancers & Rebels: How to Thrive as an Independent Creative

Copyright © Business Expert Press, LLC, 2021.

Cover design by Tamsin Baker

Interior design by Exeter Premedia Services Private Ltd., Chennai, India

First published in 2021 by
Business Expert Press, LLC
222 East 46th Street, New York, NY 10017
www.businessexpertpress.com

ISBN-13: 978-1-95334-976-7 (paperback)
ISBN-13: 978-1-95334-977-4 (e-book)

Business Expert Press Entrepreneurship and Small Business Management Collection

Collection ISSN: 1946-5653 (print)
Collection ISSN: 1946-5661 (electronic)

First edition: 2021

10 9 8 7 6 5 4 3 2 1

Dedicated to my siblings.

Description

Many creative founders and freelancers share a longing for connection, reassurance and motivation.

In this book I've interviewed inspiring, brave and creative experts across the UK and US, tapping into some incredible insights and pulling them together into this friendly guide, to offer that support which we all need from time to time.

This book's for you if you've stopped feeling 'hungry' for new client work, you're starting up for the first (or second or third!) time, or you've simply run out of steam. My intention is to offer a wealth of ideas and fresh perspectives to inspire you at any stage of your independent creative career.

Keywords

startups; business; entrepreneur; freelancers; creative; starting a business; self-employed; founder; thrive; coaching

Contents

Preface

I'm writing the book I would have enjoyed reading more than a decade ago when I set up on my own as a PR consultant in London, UK. I'd run teams, managed budgets, been a spokesperson on behalf of eye-watering amounts of investment and worked with intimidatingly high-profile leaders. Unfortunately, that did not equip me for starting and running my own creative operation.

When I worked inside agencies on behalf of household names with big budgets, it felt natural—even easy at times—to negotiate contracts, have tough conversations and develop creative campaigns. Yet, the same things that had felt so natural at a corporate suddenly felt foreign when I had to do them as a freelancer. Now I work daily as a coach, supporting creative freelancers and founders to fulfill their potential and enjoy the journey too. My clients are all incredibly talented and resourceful, but many share a longing for connection, reassurance, support and motivation.

Over my two-year writing journey, I've interviewed inspiring, brave and creative people across the UK and United States, tapping into some incredible insights and pulling them together into this friendly guide, to offer that support that we all need from time to time.

This book's for you if you've stopped feeling hungry for new client work, you're starting up for the first (or second or third!) time or you've simply run out of steam. My intention is to offer a wealth of ideas and fresh perspectives to inspire you at any stage of your independent creative career.

I truly believe—like Julia Cameron—that all people are creative and can be creative. However, I've particularly aimed these pages at those of us who already feel the need and desire to put our creative ideas and work out into the world, or have somehow contracted ourselves into being creative *on demand* almost every day, which is a tough number. I'm thinking about the PR and advertising industries, actors and presenters, artists across all media, writers, makers and anyone who works in a slightly unconventional way. You know who you are.

I'd love to hear from you all, and continue to document and share your inspiring stories and insights. This is, for me, just the start of an ongoing two-way conversation, and it's one I'd like to keep alive every day. I'm looking forward to meeting you all.

Acknowledgments

Anne Brichto, you are an unending source of inspiration, food, literature and laughter.

Sharon Wheeler, my warmest thanks and appreciation to you for reading every word of my draft manuscript and offering objective and thoughtful edits. I am so grateful to you. I understand you were paying forward a similar favor and I hope to be able to pay forward your support very soon to another author. Let's keep this going.

Becky Matthews, I truly value both your friendship and insight.

Charlotte Bailey, for your ongoing encouragement, support, good heart and cat pictures.

Eleanor Goold, for motivating me with sound and inspiring advice, when I lost my mojo.

Peter Beckett, for telling me what my book was about when I wasn't entirely sure, and organizing my messy thoughts into a coherent structure.

Fiona Chow, for your perfect combination of surrogate tiger mom and shoulder to cry on as required.

Dan Simon, for letting me delve into your incredible brain and for your high levels of enthusiasm.

Gina Cobbold, for creating space for me to write in beautiful Alicante and recommending Big Magic to me (by Elizabeth Gilbert), you really got me unstuck.

Mark Southern, for somehow getting me to write 1,000 words a day for a month in addition to my day job.

Amanda Holly, who transcribed the majority of these interviews, you are amazing.

Tamsin Baker, for being magical.

My clients, for encouraging me and cheerleading me on this journey.

Zoe Hawkins and Gillian Maxwell Carter, for holding my head together. I am very lucky to know you both.

Becky Slack, who's been a wonderful informal mentor to me through this process, thank you so much.

Introduction

Seeking freedom: Find flexibility, balance and your sense of purpose

The freelance market and gig economy are growing and thriving, with the annual *Freelancing in America* survey[1] offering optimistic findings and predictions[2] for an industry that it values at almost one trillion U.S. dollars—nearly 5 percent of U.S. GDP.

While working for yourself can be associated with uncertainty, there's also a tremendous amount of flexibility, freedom and opportunity for those bold enough to grab it. There's the lure of remote working, control over your client base and the chance to build the lifestyle you aspire to, so it's an enticing route for those brave and savvy souls who embrace it.

For the creative individual, freelancing or running your own business can offer the freedom to allow creativity to flow and to nurture and cultivate it—whether that's about exploring and experimenting with different media, seeking inspiration in fresh places or the chance to choose clients whose ethos resonates with your own. All of this can be extremely empowering. And yet, left to our own devices, we can sometimes find ourselves too far off course, and that's where a little coaching—or a few timely tips—can help us refocus and regroup.

Having worked with hundreds of freelancers and founders over the years, and set up online communities connecting thousands of freelancers—with one another and with clients—I have brought together some of the key ingredients needed to create a thriving independent, creative career. I have also interviewed experts on some of the vital issues facing creative freelancers and founders, both the practical and

---

[1] https://upwork.com/blog/2019/10/freelancing-in-america-2019/
[2] https://upwork.com/press/2019/10/03/freelancing-in-america-2019/

existential factors, which may influence artists, writers and other creatives forging their own path right now.

Firstly, I know it helps to have an appetite and hunger for working in a different way to the default employee role that most of us are raised to expect.

That hunger and drive can help you through the lean times as well as the busy, abundant months. The term feast or famine is often associated with freelance life, and while a creative spark and appetite can drive your career, developing strong boundaries and a calm confidence will be your armor in the long term.

You may be coming to this book as a long-time freelancer or founder who wants to begin a new chapter, or maybe you're flirting with the idea of setting up on your own and not even sure if it's for you. Some of us find freelancing and consultancy because we got made redundant, or are looking for a lifestyle change, other times, it finds us and we begin our freelance life around a project or client request. Whichever path you took to get here, I'm glad you're here, and I hope you never look back and are able to build the life you truly want and deserve.

CHAPTER 1

Prepare to thrive

Hunger, curiosity and creativity

Creative people who are driven by their passion, curiosity and hunger can make amazing freelancers. We can also make very insecure freelancers who strive to create the most beautiful art, write an incredibly moving piece of prose, or compose the tune that becomes legendary. If you're a creative person seeking to make a living from your art (which could be writing, ideas generation, photography, music . . . any number of skills), then your passion can propel you forward and drive you. It can also sometimes get in the way. The key is striking a balance between your motivation and what your client wants and needs. It's also about finding the sweet spot where everyone's goals meet or align, and then replicating this in a sustainable way that enables you to pay your bills, enjoy your life and embrace the freedom of freelancing without lurching from famine to feast and back again.

When you're setting out for the first time and starting to build your client base, then working out what drives you can really help you to stay motivated during the journey. It can also be handy to check in with that drive and motivation and work out if it's a healthy motivation, and—if it is—plan how to feed and nurture it and keep yourself on track. And, if it doesn't feel healthy—for example, if it is fueled by fear—then doing some work to unpick that, for example, with a coach, can be useful to help you create a strong foundation for your career.

Katy Cowan runs the online magazine and podcast *Creative Boom* and is a huge advocate of creative people building their own businesses, working freelance and following their passion. She says:

Often the hardest part of becoming a freelancer is taking that first step, as so much feels uncertain. But if I were to tell you that not even a full-time job is secure, would that change your perspective? We shouldn't glorify freelancing, as it's not for everyone. However, for those who do want to start a business, it's advisable to build a safety net and develop more contacts before going solo. The first couple of years will also be tough—but once you have some regular clients and you've established a reputation, you'll find the work keeps coming. You'll wonder why you didn't go freelance sooner. And if it doesn't work out? I tell myself I can always get a job again. But it's been 13 years since I started my own business.

Katy identifies some of the biggest fears that prevent people from going freelance:

- Fear of the unknown
- Not having enough work
- Not having enough money
- Not being good enough
- Not having a good work/life balance
- Fear of the competition
- Fear of the economic climate

The fears Katy identifies from her experience of running *Creative Boom* are exactly the same fears that my coaching clients bring to me almost every day too—whether that is in person, by e-mail or phone, or on the online forums I have run and been part of. At what point will these fears not exist for every freelancer? The same fears tend to affect a huge majority of freelancers throughout their careers. And, while this may not feel terribly reassuring, it also means that there is often no 'right time' to go out on your own, win new clients and be a huge success, and there is no better or worse time to fail trying either. Economic downturns can be an opportunity for independent consultants as much as they can be a challenge. Wherever you are starting from, that is where you are at and you can begin to move forward from that place to get closer to feeling fulfilled in your career.

Let's unpack those fears a little bit further and explore them in more detail:

Fear of the unknown, while it can be a concern, can also be a motivator and drive us forward in our creative journey. Think about how fear feels . . . perhaps your heart races, maybe you get a bit giddy, it might feel hard to focus. Now think about how excitement feels: Racing heart? Giddy? Finding focus a challenge? Perhaps, fear of the unknown is also excitement about what might be around the corner. Excitement about that *ping* as someone buys one of your products online or a new business enquiry lands in your inbox.

The fear of scarcity and not having enough work or money is a practical and realistic fear. The reliability of having an employer and a contract can certainly feel safer than freelancing.

As a founder or freelancer, putting some security in place, where it is lacking, can be vital. This could come from a number of sources and examples might include:

- Putting insurances in place such as loss of income or health insurance.
- Creating a budget and a financial plan and working with an accountant and financial advisor to future-proof your business.
- Having a number of sources of income is also an option, so for example, a freelance writer may have a mixture of copywriting and strategy work, run courses, paid speaking slots and might also rent out their spare room. As long as you are able to find balance, it is possible to create a portfolio career. I have friends who run a canoe center and also sell Christmas trees, among various other successful enterprises. This may sound like two unconnected businesses, but they have land and when the water is frozen and canoeing is not possible, then the other business comes into focus for a few weeks of the year.
- Having a 'Plan B'. This is something I talk about with my financial advisor. She checks in with me once in a while and we make sure that my actual circumstances and what I had anticipated are still matching up. If they are not, we might revert to Plan B for a while. Having someone pragmatic like

that can really help—I'd describe her as head over heart (in a business sense) and myself as the opposite. For me, it's vital to have someone so practical on hand when I get a bit dreamy and idealistic. Although she has a huge heart too!

These are simply a few examples and you will of course have your own ways of locking in some security. The freelancers and founders who worry about security and do not do something about it are the ones who will feel the pain if their clients do pull back. And the worry itself is simply a reminder that you need to address this, a bit like an alarm clock on snooze, the worry will keep popping up until we find a resolution!

The freelance fear of not being 'good enough' works on two levels. There is the aspect of your actual skills and what you may wish to do to brush those up in terms of learning and development, and then the more psychological fear of not being good enough in terms of 'worthiness'. The first one is more easily addressed with an audit to work out where the gaps might be and creating a personal development plan for yourself, costing it out and ascertaining what the next step is (and how much it might cost in time or money). The second is a more in-depth dialogue that may happen with your coach, therapist or simply through journaling or other forms of self-reflection.

Not having a great work/life balance is often a reason people go freelance in the first place. But, if it's your tendency to work hard and be a perfectionist, this can be a problem that follows you around if you do not address it! Notice what your go-to behavior is when you are really up against it and if working all the hours or perfectionism crop up, then perhaps this trend was not about the role you did before but about who you are as a person and how you respond to pressure. Bringing old behaviors into a new role is not always helpful.

Putting strong boundaries in place and also checking in with yourself by completing an exercise known as the 'Wheel of Life' from time to time can help show up where your life and work are out of balance, allowing you to reconnect to the under-loved aspects of your wheel. So, for example, you may discover that work is getting so much of your time that your health is suffering. And, being aware of that, and creating a plan around how to re-balance it could help you to focus more at work, and make the time you spend there more valuable, as well as the obvious benefit of better physical and mental health. Search online for 'Wheel of Life' to find templates and instructions on how to go about this.

Now, to be clear I'm not saying leave your job with no financial security, plan or preparation—quite the opposite. But, wherever you are in your journey, if a flexible creative life is calling you, then it is highly unlikely that someone will arrive at your door, or tap you on the shoulder and tell you now is the time to begin! This isn't a fairy tale. If you want magic in your world, you might have to bring it yourself. And, planning how to do that is either the first step or the start of your growth plan if you're already freelancing and looking for more income, freedom and success.

If you're a creative freelancer relying on your career for financial security (as most of us do), then the start of your journey may seem especially daunting. But, what you need to get going can simply be boiled down to one word! There is one thing that you need more than a beautiful business card, fancy website or groovy logo to get you started on your journey, or to grow. It's *clients*. Clients, clients, clients.

I learned this from my photographer friend Jon, in my first week of freelancing—in fact, he pretty much bellowed it down the phone to me. I was chatting enthusiastically about my plans to start working for myself and how I needed a logo and a website and so on. And he stopped me in my tracks and told me the only thing I needed to get started on my journey was at least one client and that without a client I did not have a business.

He was right of course. Unless you have some investment or savings, then a logo and business cards are a luxury to schedule into your plan for Month 1. They are not essential during your first week and if you prioritize these things, there simply won't be any money in your business bank account to pay for them with. For me, the first step is to work out how to get your first client, what service or product you will offer to them and how much you will charge them. Create a short-term plan around that goal. Then go get that client.

This will of course require a strong sense of self-motivation and drive. Other personality traits that will really enhance your freelance journey include:

- A keen sense of curiosity and a willingness to ask questions
- An appetite for listening and learning
- A thick skin and a sense of ease around giving and receiving feedback

Agile PR: A start-up story

Sometimes a business is born through 'fear and necessity'. It's not always part of a beautiful strategic plan. Although luckily for Rachel Picken, who uses these two words to describe how she got going, she is rather talented at thinking on her feet:

Rachel runs Agile PR, an independent consultancy based in Cornwall, UK. She specializes in strategic public relations (PR) consultancy, training and mentoring for PR and integrated marketing and copywriting. A twist in her business is that she works with Agile project management methodologies, delivering training courses and writing about Agile application at organizations nationally and internationally.

Agile, as Rachel explained to me, is a project management and workflow methodology that started out in the software industry in 2001. It focuses on delivering value quickly and regularly, rather than project success being defined by delivery on time and on budget.

It has since been applied to a broader range of industries outside of the software world.

Rachel explains what prompted her to begin working as an independent consultant:

Fear and necessity! But also realising it was the very best option to me as a working single mother. I split up with my husband at the end of 2015, and we ran a business together, so within six months I had to move house, leave a marriage and a business, and of course a job that I loved and was actually good at.

Initially I did a phased exit from the business, but it became clear that I needed a clean break. I had been offered teaching work delivering diploma and advanced certificate courses for the Chartered Institute of Public Relations (CIPR). It was the baseline income I needed to take that step. So after coffee and some encouragement with a professional friend, I set up as a sole trader. My boyfriend at the time was also a very successful freelance crisis comms PR, so I could see the opportunities to fit a great career around my life and home.

It wasn't plain sailing at the start and around a year in, Rachel told me she did apply for two jobs when things got a bit quiet. That experience in itself gave her a knock-back too: she recalls that she didn't even get called for an interview, which she remembers thinking was really odd because she was known to the company. The other job Rachel applied for, as an alternative to running her business, led her through to the interview stage, but she didn't get this either. She remembers crying her eyes out when she got the call, but she says it forced her to make her business work. And, she picked herself up and carried on growing and developing Agile PR.

Now Rachel earns the equivalent of 'a really good salary', while working three to four days per week and being flexible around her two daughters, aged seven and ten. She can also prioritize herself and her health—some days she could be at the gym or a workout class, having a meeting or holding a workshop, then going on the school run or volunteering for the class bake sale. She's essentially designed her business and life to prioritize the things she is great at and loves doing and works incredibly hard but with space for her family too, demonstrating the sort of balance she can help her clients to achieve, as she does so. She said:

Interestingly, the MD of the business where I applied but didn't get an interview messaged me on LinkedIn to invite me to apply for a job . . . pretty much the same job I'd applied for previously. The candidate hadn't worked out. I was flattered and did consider it for a moment, but said thanks but no thanks. It was full time hours, and as the MD herself recognized, I was being rewarded by "rowing my own boat." I've since set Agile PR up as a limited company, and

I'm exploring opportunities to grow without compromising my work/ life balance.

I asked Rachel what she knows now that would have helped her get started as a freelancer:

That cashflow really is king. When you are the sole person responsible for keeping a roof over your head, and a client is slow to pay or you have a quiet patch, it can get a bit hairy. Also—I have some really huge, internationally renowned clients in the university/ higher education sector, and I have really small start-up and charity clients. The smaller clients can often be the better payers, because you establish a relationship with the person paying your invoice. So it's good to mix it up a bit. I once waited about four months for invoices to be paid from one big client because they had changed their finance systems. I was one of a number of suppliers to get lost in the system.

The freelancers who are truly "adulting" are the ones who have 6–12 months of income saved in the bank before they start. I just didn't have that luxury. However one thing I really recommend is mapping out your projects and clients, particularly if you don't have retained clients. Be generous with your day rates, and don't fix your model in a way where you are billing for every day you work. You need admin days, marketing days, training, and let's face it—holidays!

The best piece of advice I got was from a recruitment specialist called Liz Gadd. She was the one who encouraged me to go it alone and put myself at the top of my list of priorities.

"How do I start to win work?" I said.

"Make a prospect list," she replied. "30-50 names of people you'd like to work with."

So on my first day, sat at my desk in my bedroom, that's what I did. I brainstormed contacts and people I liked or old clients, and I got in touch with them one by one. Hand-on-heart, about 30 percent of the people on that list that I contacted, I generated work with. I did this again earlier this year when I was staring down the barrel of little work—and it quickly filled up my schedule again.

We also discussed what has been Rachel's biggest lifesaver since going freelance:

Having a real niche which has enabled me to make a name for myself in a very specific area. It's opened me up to global clients—for example, I write long-form features for the Scrum Alliance (based in Colorado) for their magazine and website.

Also, my shared office space. I pay a monthly fee to have a desk in a coworking space near where I live. The office is owned by a music distribution company so there is always a killer playlist on, great coffee, it's dog-friendly and the people are lovely. Ultimately it's about community—everyone is so supportive and we celebrate each other's successes, collaborate on clients but also act as a sounding board for each other. That is invaluable.

The quest for self-actualization

Building your client base and maintaining healthy cash flow are the main priorities for most of us. But, for some artists, the primary focus is on being the best they can and putting art out into the world, regardless of the shackles of clients and money.

One such artist is the painter David McAdam Freud, son of the artist Lucian Freud, who explained to me what it means to create art from his unique perspective:

For me, being an artist is being free of financial motivations or the wish to have a job. I decide or agree that something is going to be made, hope it will appear without my consciously inventing it then compromise between manipulation and play while exploring the idea of the thing and its existence—texture, smell, shape, weight, taste, intention, effect it has on the space surrounding it. I try to hold at bay any thoughts of cost, marketability of the piece, acceptance by whomever commissioned it, as I think these considerations distract

from the work but they inevitably occur and, if I am not very careful,
overwhelm the process.

While David's motivation and drive flies in the face of what most
business books tell you, I'm writing this with an awareness that paying
the bills is not always the 'be-all and end-all' of our creative endeavors.
I'd like to leave our minds open to the possibility that sometimes—if not
always—we work to create because it feels good to do so, not simply to
pay the rent.

I spoke about this with Eszter Iván, who's a UK-based dance movement psychotherapist, psychologist and coach. We talked about Maslow's
hierarchy of needs, a diagram and popular theory by American psychologist Abraham Maslow (1943, 1954). His famous pyramid diagram displays a five-tier model of human needs, with those deemed the most basic
and physiological (such as food and water) at the base of the pyramid and
those at the top, being more psychological such as self-esteem.

Eszter and I discussed how the top internal motivation is
self-actualization: to become the most we can be—which includes
self-fulfillment and personal growth—and how important this is if we
think about becoming or being a whole person. She works with dancers and specializes in movement. Eszter emphasized the importance of
balance and self-care, especially for those of us who are driven to create
and fulfill our potential. In general, a balance between living to work and
working to live is where most of us are likely to be. She said:

> For me it is about finding the right soil and environment for the seed
> to grow. It is hard work to find that! Self-actualization will happen
> only if there is passion, energy and possibility to flourish using our
> skills and learning within the process.
>
> As founders or freelancers, we must remember that we are managing
> ourselves as well. We are our own leaders. We need to make sure we
> value each step and everything that we do, not just think about big
> milestones which we want to reach, but see the journey and enjoy the
> journey. I think it's so easy to forget this when our internal dialogue
> might be: 'OK I need more money, I need more appliances' and so on.

Whether your goal is making money, self-actualization or something else, keep connecting back with *why* you are doing what you do. Explore the things that motivate and drive you and what you are hungry for. This will put some gas in your tank for your freelance or founder journey. Having a clear awareness of where you're heading can help forward momentum, particularly on difficult days.

Build a business you believe in

- Choose what you stand for
- Be aware of what motivates you
- Decide what you want to spend more or less time doing

One of the most joyful parts of running your own business or being a creative freelancer or consultant is the opportunity to build a business you truly believe in. To position what's important to you firmly at the core of your operation—whether that's amazing customer service, a passion for the environment, or the desire to build a multi-national business that turns over millions. Many people start their freelance career or business by answering an advert for a short-term contract, or responding to a request for ad-hoc support. Then they go where the work is, and that's how they find their first client. While this is a legitimate way to make a living, creative people who take this approach on a long-term basis can end up feeling despondent, finding themselves working at the whims of a mixed bag of clients and not being truly happy or congruent with what's important to them. I was lucky to be head-hunted for my first freelance role with a government department, and I do say it was luck rather than judgment, as I had a very vague and incomplete plan at the time. What I had done though, by way of preparation for starting out on my own, was to meet with people who I respected in the communications industry and ask them for advice and feedback, which I took on board, and I also gathered testimonials and recommendations from the most influential and well-connected individuals in my network. I'd suggest you start doing the same, even if you're not yet sure if running a business is for you.

As a coach, I advocate working backwards. Start with a clear picture of where you want to end up, and map out a path that takes you there.

The most important part is to *start* from where you are now, not from some future version of yourself, but with you as you are today. Build the business that you wish to work for and in. And, begin doing this when it is just you. It is entirely possible to have a company culture even when the company consists of one individual. So, for starters, rather than choosing any client, at any price, think about the power of having the right client as your starting point and what can lead on from that.

The first step to building your new brand can be about acknowledging and tuning into your beliefs and values to establish exactly what it is you stand for—getting to the essence of you. And, if you have a business partner, then do this for both of you and find out where the overlaps are.

At the start-up phase, give yourself permission to ask for the help you need. I've been involved in a few startups over the years and I've found people tend to be incredibly generous in letting you 'pick their brains' for half an hour, whether that is on legal advice, branding, human resources (HR), or something else. Being a startup is a great chance to get some really good professional advice, and then pay it forward when you have the chance by doing the same for others. And, yes you can speak to me for half an hour free of charge if you are thinking of starting up. That is absolutely okay.

CHAPTER 2

What do you stand for?

Define your brand and
understand your values

If you've never asked yourself this question before—*what do I stand for?*—then it might be handy for us to unpack what we mean by beliefs and values before we think about how it affects the start or growth phase of our freelance or start-up journey.

Zoe Hawkins is a coach who trains other coaches. I turned to her to find out more about how she defines beliefs and values. This is what she told me:

We are all driven by our unique values. Values are things that are important to us and need to be met in order to experience fulfilment. Everyone's values are different and they are shaped by our early experiences and influences in our lives. This can explain why some people choose to go down the corporate route, and others choose to work for themselves. For example, a value such as freedom may be easier to meet when you work for yourself and have full control over the work that you do, when and where you do it.

Additionally, it is common for people to reach a phase in their lives where they crave more meaning. In our early careers many people choose the corporate route as a way to earn money, perhaps to buy a house and build their security. Once basic needs are met it gives space for other needs to emerge, such as giving back, helping others, or exploring aspects of themselves that they haven't felt they've had time for. You can take more risks when you have a strong foundation of security. It can be at this time of life that people make big career changes such as becoming a writer or an artist.

Understanding your values and whether you are currently fulfilling them or not could be one of the vital keys to your happiness levels in your freelance career. Once you have done some exploratory work around defining what they are (which you may wish to do with the help of a coach or another business person), then you are in a stronger position to work out how to embed them—whether you are setting up from scratch or refocusing your existing role.

A simple starting point that Zoe explained to me is to create a long list of words of possible values such as *religion, power, friendship, spontaneity, creativity, sexuality, compassion* and circle or cross out the ones that resonate with you. Add new words and see where it takes you. Then, you may wish to go further and explore what's behind your belief . . . ask yourself (or get your coach or mentor to ask you) why that value is important to you and see if actually there is another significant meaning behind that which you'd like to bring to the fore.

When you are happy you have discovered your core values, you may wish to prioritize them before looking at how to embed them into your days, weeks and months—and into your business. Some may be easy to implement straight away, while others could be future ambitions and part of a timeline of goals for the next year, or even five years. Remember they are personal to your business and do not have to reflect what you see others doing—in fact, having *different* goals and values than other founders can be a huge asset, as demonstrated by small business owner Rich Leigh, who runs a PR business in England, UK. Rich recognized what was important to him and his staff and made a drastic change to the workstyle of his agency. In 2018, he introduced the four-day working week across his business, *Radioactive PR*.

Rich's brave and thoughtful change took significant preparation and planning to achieve his goals of:

- Better staff retention
- Lower rates of absence
- Increased staff and client happiness
- Lower levels of stress

Rich implemented a trial of the four-day working week after consulting with clients and staff, and when that went well, he used his tech knowledge to streamline communication and reporting processes, slightly reduce holiday allocations, and give staff a whopping 40 days back to themselves in return for losing just five days holiday a year. Rich also makes sure that clients can call on him or the team in emergencies. He explained:

When speaking to marketing/brand directors in the past, one of the main reasons cited for leaving an agency/freelance relationship is the lack of communication, unless things are going well—odd when we consider ourselves to be good communicators. It turns out though that most PR people think communicating means sending results, whereas for us, especially since I started using WhatsApp groups with near-enough every client, it's more about day-to-day updates. On what's being worked on, on what's been asked for, on planning, on reactive opportunities, and then, of course, on results. Clients just want to feel in the know, and to feel like everything is on track to be delivered, to the best of our combined abilities—especially when the alternative to hiring an agency is developing the in-house team.

Our client/agency relationships have definitely been made stronger since starting the four-day week, not least because I—and we—are incredibly conscious of the need to constantly communicate. Not that we weren't before, but it's one of the two main factors I asked for feedback on both during and after the six-week trial I implemented nearly a year ago—asking them to score us both on communication and results in surveys in light of the trial. This doesn't mean inane nonsense—although I really do feel like, within reason, our relationships with clients are far friendlier than I've ever had elsewhere—it means having something to say, and occasionally, telling the client what they might not want to hear. That a story isn't doing as well as we thought it would—so here's what we're doing about it, or that an idea of theirs might not be the best decision, in our opinion.

In terms of always being 'on', as a result of emails/WhatsApp, the four-day week has given us the chance to have that really honest conversation with clients. They know that, should they ever need us, we are there—on a Friday at midday just as much as on a Saturday at 11pm—but in highlighting some boundaries, communicating that the time they pay for will be managed well and accordingly, to achieve the results we're all after, I've found that out-of-hours chat that can wait has reduced. Of course, there'll always be a reactive opportunity that happens outside of normal hours that we can talk about, or a budding crisis a client might want to discuss, but by and large, the thoughts and concerns of clients are kept to within office hours.

And as you might expect, Rich's brave move has reaped plenty of press coverage and attention, as well as curiosity from people intrigued by the experiment and the long-term implementation of this approach.

This also shows that making a change, which is positive for your freelance operation or your business, is not always about doing more of something, it could just as easily be about stopping something or doing less. The first step is to review what you'd like to change and explore what might be possible, with an open mind.

The other powerful lesson that leapt out at me from Rich's experiment is how essential it is to tune in to what's important to you and make that the core of your brand. If you truly believe in those differentiators—what makes your business different or even unique compared to competitors—then it hopefully won't feel like a chore to market yourself, in fact it will feel authentic and natural. Rich's clear passion for, and belief in, the four-day working week has been a thread running through his business's communications and stands for much more than just days on the calendar. It is about trust and boundaries, freedom and open communication, about being brave and trying something different and also about evaluation and feedback. All of these elements are key to running a successful operation and yet by doing this so openly and bravely, Rich has also gained plenty of positive news coverage for his idea. Not only is this well-deserved, but it also demonstrates the power of "show don't tell"—a phrase I often use in coaching when explaining the difference between *saying* you have these values and actually *living* them. Rich lives his values, and if we can too, then we can hit our flow.

Set your goals

Setting goals will guide you in running your freelance business and in pitching for, managing and reporting on your client work too. If no one knows where they are aiming, then it is incredibly hard to know if it's going well.

When you set goals for yourself, or for a client project, then make sure they are *SMART—specific, measurable, achievable, realistic and timebound.* And be aware of whether you are relying on anyone else to bring those goals to life or whether they are 100 percent within your control. That can seriously affect your chances of success.

If you don't yet have a client base, or contracts, then your goals are likely to be around generating new business, creating a structure and bringing those new clients on board. Having a realistic and true under-standing of the nature of the industry you're working in can be vital when you set your goals.

Highs and lows

Alexis Hightower lives in New York, and explained to me how her career has hit some incredible peaks. Yet she does not take that for granted or underestimate the need for us as creative people, to stretch ourselves in order to reach our goals:

I've always been musical and started performing at a very young age. I would say my professional career began in earnest immediately after I finished college, so at the age of 21. That's actually late by enter-tainment business standards, but college was a non-negotiable in my household and I did not get a degree in music.

The "highs" are two-fold really. Possibly the biggest high for me was performing my original music in front of 5,000 peo-ple at a San Sebastian music festival in Spain while opening for

Bobby McFerrin. That was otherworldly and really stands out. I performed with the late, great Roy Hargrove's Big Band, opened for Gil Scott-Heron, performed as Mimi in the Broadway tour of "Rent" and I've taken my band all over the world. These are all highlights and are very precious to me. Of course, getting a coveted booking or getting a song placed in a film or other medium, is totally thrilling. Anytime you get to a "yes" it just feels good. The other type of high is connected to the process of being creative. Each day that I get to wake up and write, sing, create, practise, is truly a dream come true. Each moment that I get to spend working at my craft is a high unto itself. It also means that I continually improve because I get to put the time into doing what I love rather than say, going to work in an office or shop all day every day.

I think a career in music and arts is always characterized by highs and lows. It's really just the nature of the industry. There's a saying that "you're only as good as your last fill-in-the-blank." It's not like the corporate world where once you reach a certain level and, generally, you stay there. The entertainment world stays being precipitous. Even the Beyoncés of the world have to constantly compete and stretch themselves in order to maintain their status at 'the top.'

Figure out what helps you to thrive

I could tell you to never work in your pajamas or to always sit at a desk in an ergonomic seating position—and while this might be great for your posture, only you can truly know what helps you to work at your best. Whether you need a standing desk, outdoor space, a pot plant or an office dog is up for you to decide, *but* do decide—my one piece of advice on your freelance office is not to leave it to chance or the default option. When you're thinking about your values and what drives you, consider what you physically need to operate well. And what you would like to look at and surround yourself with. And I'd encourage you to be incredibly honest with yourself, in truth very few of us really work at our very best in bed—but if you're someone who does then I'm not planning to stand in your way!

It can be surprisingly difficult to admit to ourselves what it is that we need—not because we don't know, but because it's often the *boring* stuff. I spent a year of my life going to bed at midnight (or later) and getting up at 5.30 a.m., fueled by strong morning coffees and enjoying beers every evening from the brewery where I worked. It was a fun year and a fantastic experience. But in reality, I'm aware that eight hours sleep, little or no alcohol, little or no caffeine, and a walk outside is a hell of a lot better for me than the brewery year was. I'd never have got this book started, let alone finished, if I was still immersed in the lifestyle I chose then.

Where you work from—and how you get there

As freelancers or small business owners, we have the freedom to mix it up a little. We could operate from a co-working space one day, a cafe the next and from home another day. Bear in mind confidentiality and what you need to work well. While being a digital nomad is a dream for many, the amount of people I hear having clearly private work conversations on public transport is surprising. If you want to work from a different location, think about what you need to make that possible. For example, it could be as simple as a pair of headphones, or downloading a piece of software so you can access your files when you're not at home. Whatever it is, make it easy for yourself to work in the way that motivates and suits you the most.

If you are unsure about what sort of environment you need to thrive, then spend some time really exploring that and setting up a workspace that helps you to feel motivated, organized, comfortable, happy and productive. This is likely to mean different things for different people. Some clients have plastered their wall with charts and plans, others are minimalist and others have a garden office, to designate *home* and *work*. I loved working out of *Huckletree* when I was in London; not only did they provide flexible co-working space, there was also the added bonus of networking with other innovative small businesses sharing the space as well as an ethos that fitted with mine. They really thought about environmental factors and even the desks were made from reclaimed materials that had previously been used in film sets. Why film sets? Well apart from being a cool fact, it was also a link to one of the founder's other roles as an actor. The space had plenty of open-plan desks and meeting areas, as well as private rooms for calls and conversations. And it was located centrally, which, I admit, I found impressive when inviting clients in. If you are looking for a co-working space, I'd advise looking beyond the price and the address, as although these can be important factors, the people and the space itself, plus its ethos and values can really help you create your company culture too.

When you work

I've spoken to hundreds of freelancers over the years, and most are in tune with when they work best but many seem to also work against that hardwired instinct. I'd suggest going with it instead of fighting it. For example, if you truly operate best in the evening, consider working with overseas clients who will be online at the same time as you are at your peak. Or if you know you need boundaries around your evenings and weekends, please stop replying to your clients at evenings and weekends. Consider instead setting up an *out of office* message that reminds clients of your opening hours. Eventually you may be able to switch it off; you are training yourself as much as you are training them.

If you work for yourself and spend a lot of time at home or have a home office, then poor boundaries around when work begins and ends can be a huge pitfall, especially if you work with a partner, as I used to. Is it acceptable to chat about work over dinner? Could that be a great use of time or is it polluting your homelife? There is no right answer, instead of saying how it *should* be done, I'd suggest creating boundaries that work for you and then sticking with them, adapting them if they are not working and talking about them together. Even if your partner does not work with you formally, if your office is based at home, it might still be worth having a conversation about where the boundaries lie. Just because you are there more often might not mean that you want to do more chores than your partner who is perhaps out at work. Or perhaps they don't really want your notes spilling across the kitchen table at night. These are simple examples, and of course, it might run a lot deeper. Signaling the *end of the working day* can be an important ritual too. It might be an action that you do—such as for me turning on the radio and starting to cook a meal (I love preparing food), or it could be a time of the day that signals the end of work—we used to finish at 6 every day, except Friday, in my agency, and on Friday, we'd finish at 5.10 when the same song was always played on the radio each week. A little ritual and a little reward too, an early finish for the whole team.

How you work

What do I mean by this? Well, a lot of people start working for themselves either using the same systems they used when they had a boss or no systems at all. So, for example, when I first started coaching, I was taking payments into my bank account and setting up meetings via e-mail, or text, and then sometimes someone would message me on social media at the weekend, to arrange a session or change some appointments, and of course, this wasn't ideal. This wasn't a system and didn't work well for me or my clients.

Now I'm not saying I have it *right*, but what works a lot better for me now is clients buying my time in advance through my website and logging in to set up their own appointments. My assistant is on hand to help if the software is confusing or an appointment needs altering at short notice, but in general, I have set up a *serve yourself* system, and it puts clients in control. I have also chosen software that syncs automatically with my calendar and so, it notices if I have another appointment or have blocked time out and ensures that I am not double-booked. When mistakes happen, they tend to be my human error and not the system. If I stick to the system, it works really well. I found it felt uncomfortable at first to tell people I couldn't arrange sessions via social media messages, especially as I do market my services via social platforms. But I have become so used to taking the conversation off social media and into my work inbox that it feels natural now.

When thinking about how you work, consider whether the systems and processes you use (if any) are serving you well. Do a bit of an audit and you may find that you can free up time and brain space by trialing a different approach.

I have found my clients to be incredibly supportive of me when I've tried new systems, as long as they are built with the client in mind too and not just for my own convenience of course.

Who do you need around you to thrive?

While you are auditing your systems and processes, it may be incredibly helpful to audit some of the relationships you have around you at work. This could range from whether your accountant is helpful to looking at those people who have always supported you and who you may not have noticed too much before. Plus, inevitably, some people will be energy drains.

If you notice that a client or supplier really depletes your energy, do consider what the options might be. Equally, if there are people who always fill you with energy and life and inspire you, then maybe think about how you can bring them into your world a bit more. I love to bring inspiring and supportive people together at breakfast events. We have a loose agenda and theme and listen to each other, making connections and enjoying the energy the event creates. I choose to hold these at lovely locations, so that even when we walk in, before we have actually even started the meeting, we feel inspired.

CHAPTER 3

Being productive

Maintain forward momentum and motivation

Dr. Gabija Toleikyte, PhD, has studied the brain extensively and I was excited to speak to her about the scientific reasons that we sometimes hold back or lack momentum, even when we know what we'd like to achieve. A lot of my clients recognize their tendency to self-sabotage, or to lose momentum and lack self-belief, and one of the reasons for this, I learned, can stem from our brains trying to keep us safe from perceived danger. She said:

There's a part of the brain called the amygdala—which is pretty much there to protect us from danger—and it's really ancient, in that dogs, cats, cows and rodents have very similar amygdalas.

Now our amygdala hates unpredictability, hates change and hates a lack of certainty. So when we talk about people who are self-employed, who don't know where their next piece of work is coming from, or people who don't know whether they will be creative enough to do something and who really can't guarantee things, the amygdala gets active and it changes the way we are and the way we think. Our amygdala's job is to prepare our body to escape danger.

So our amygdala isn't there to make us really creative and make really sound rational decisions, the opposite is true. The amygdala's connected to the rational brain centre, called the pre-frontal cortex, at the front of the brain, and it reduces activity there, so when our amygdala's activated, we become less rational. There are a lot of irrational fears and irrational thoughts that can surface—a lot of past trauma can come to the surface—even something that might feel completely irrelevant. So for example, if your art teacher criticized you when you were a child, it might seem ridiculous to care about it at this point as an adult if you're an artist, but when our amygdala's active it will remember all the past hurt of a similar kind.

So when we think about self-belief, every single one of us, when we do something we really love, and we get really absorbed and get in that state of flow, we don't care about self-belief. It only matters when our amygdala triggers, or is triggered, we need almost to prove ourselves, our amygdala is almost like the devil's advocate, and we can say: 'oh I need to believe myself enough to prove to my amygdala that I can do it.' So that's one way of doing it, but the second way of doing it is actually to soothe the amygdala, to calm the amygdala down. And in my experience with my clients, and personally and through the literature of my research, some things I find that help our amygdala to calm down are really quite basic.

Slowing down the breathing, and doing daily breathing activities, even as simple as breathe in to the count of four, hold to the count of four, breathe out to the count of four, and do that four times. It's a very simple formula, but even that gives amygdala a sense of safety. The reason being that when there isn't a physical threat we have time to breathe and focus on breathing, whereas if we allow ourselves to breathe really fast and hard, it further reinforces to our amygdala that there is danger.

This *fight or flight* instinct kicking in can be a real deal-breaker for us when we want to create momentum for ourselves. Noticing our triggers and finding ways to soothe ourselves can help many of us to overcome the *stuckness*. It can be valuable to try a few techniques to find out what works for you, rather than replicating another person's exact routine. Here are a few ideas that you might like to try, based on Dr. Gabija's expertise. She advises starting with small steps and creating healthy daily habits when you feel good, rather than trying these when you are experiencing stress:

- Breathing exercises
- Healthy eating/sleeping habits

- Walking in nature
- Gratitude list: this starts a dialogue with our amygdala, challenging our negative thoughts
- Charting your progress

Dr. Gabija also explained to me that our brains can go from negative self-talk straight to the opposite—a self-elated state where we start seeing fault in others. If we can, instead, cultivate a healthy mindset, and be objective about who we are and what we need, acknowledging everything is a work in progress, then we can learn and grow.

Incentivizing yourself

When you think about how you will reward yourself (and others) for a job well done, it may be worth exploring your approach to money, before you decide what your financial goals and incentives will be.

I spoke to Emma Maslin, a certified money coach and NLP practitioner in the United Kingdom, known as *The Money Whisperer*. Previously a chartered accountant, she supports her clients around building wealth, working with how people manage their emotions and subconscious beliefs around money. She explained:

I use personality profiling as part of my toolkit as a money coach. We've all got a mix of different money personality traits within us. When an opportunity presents itself, your dominant archetype will be the one you naturally lean on to enable you to make a decision. I tend to find with business owners that the nurturing trait and archetype shows up for a lot of people I work with. This personality trait is frequently one of the top three in a lot of small business owners: it's the archetype that will look after others at the expense of themselves—in business and in relationships.

Serving others is essential when you are in business, but the reality is, you need to help yourself first and then help other people. It's like putting the oxygen mask on in the plane.

For example, I worked with one client who runs a health spa. She runs the spa and employs people to provide the services for the spa.

She's got rooms around the spa that she lets out to people such as yoga teachers and holistic therapists. When she came to me she was taking a percentage of their income as her cut: so there was no motivation for the therapists to maximise their numbers because if they had just three people in she would take a cut, and they would still get their cut. She had no boundaries in place around how she charged.

So we implemented a really simple change which was for her to put clear boundaries in place which put her first. She asked for a booking fee for the room which covered her needs and her requirements to be profitable, and guaranteed her a level of income, and then the onus was on them then to market the session to cover their fixed costs. Their profit was over and above whatever they paid to her, so that actually ended up generating a lot more income for both sides. They were encouraged to get people in.

When it comes to finances you've really got to take a step back and say 'what are my needs?', 'what do I need to generate from my business to live the life I want to live?', 'why am I doing this?', 'what is my purpose?'. Then ask yourself 'are my needs met?' and only then see how you can support others once that need is met.

Accountability

While money can be an incentive and reward, some personality types are propelled forward by being accountable to someone, in addition to the clients they produce work for. Accountability can help with tasks such as the planning and promotion of your freelance business, and any other tasks that are not client-facing such as business development, and personal development or learning.

Joining a mastermind group, business group or professional body can help if you are the sort of person who enjoys being part of a team. If you are more of a solo worker, then finding a like-minded person you can check in with, or an online group, can help offer some accountability, without even leaving your desk. Keeping a progress journal or using an app to keep you on track can help to break up large tasks into manageable actions. I like MiGoals who produce 90-day progress journals—there are plenty to choose from. The method of accountability is less important than the discipline of it. Making time to do the tasks on the list is also key. One form of accountability that keeps us on track with our client work is simply the fact that we are getting paid for successful completion of it and the need to pay our bills! This is one reason why we may need greater accountability for tasks and projects that are not income-generators. And the first step is to be accountable to ourselves by creating the time and space to complete the task, before we then ask someone else to help keep us on track.

Being accountable extends to completing timesheets for client work (if required) and carving out time to focus on the running of our business. Ways that you might find helpful to carve out time can include:

- Spending less time on social media or making that time goal-orientated rather than simply browsing
- Prepping for yourself, whether that is food, tidying your desk at the end of each day or setting up reminders and systems—there are small actions you can take to save time in the future
- Being honest with yourself about tasks you don't actually need to do at all, or which can be automated

When you have cleared space in your schedule and worked out what you want to be held accountable for, try to make your goal as specific and measurable as possible. If you are looking for accountability to create a plan, tell your buddy or coach when you'll create the plan, how you will do it, what format it will take and the reward you'll give yourself when it's done.

To create and be accountable for good habits rather than one-off tasks, look out for challenges such as *Inktober* for artists, where artists use social media to create accountability for drawing/sketching every day for a month and sharing their work. This also has the benefit of being part of a community and is fun—plus the outwards accountability, in this case, sharing online, can help to promote your expertise and skill too. You may also experience positive energy from the other participants and make new friends and contacts, helping to eliminate some of the challenges of solo working, such as loneliness!

A few questions to ask yourself:

How will you reward yourself for meeting your goal(s)?

Try to include this in your plan if you can, and be as specific as possible.

So, what might a reward look like for a job well done? My freelance clients set themselves rewards ranging from a cup of coffee in the garden to a shiny new 4 × 4 vehicle. The size of the reward is usually appropriate to the size of the goal, and it can be useful to set smaller goals and rewards along the way. These do not have to tap into bad habits—so for example, they do not have to relate to sugary food, a spending splurge or a large glass of wine, but sometimes can. The reward does not have to have a monetary value; it can be something as simple as a walk on the beach or listening to your favorite song. The important factor is that you celebrate success and also recognize it in others, as it can help so much with motivation, structure and job satisfaction.

Additionally, when you do reach your goal and have that moment of celebration, it may be appropriate to mark it in other ways too, as well as your reward. These could include:

- Photos to use now or later in your marketing (with client permission of course)
- Measurement: what did you improve/change/achieve and what was the impact?
- Award entries: where your achievement is significant or noteworthy, consider entering it for an award
- Case studies: if it's appropriate, ask your client whether you can use their story in a case study, either now or in the future

What does success look like?

Clients can sometimes be vague about what success looks like. Therefore, we cannot always leave it to our clients to define success. We have to agree specifics with them and evaluate our campaigns on completion, knowing that the work has been delivered and we've earned our fee. Defining success when planning a PR campaign, for example, can be tricky as it's almost impossible to say which newspapers, magazines or TV shows will pick up the story, and so this can sometimes be used as an excuse (by clients and practitioners) for not defining the goal, but it isn't a valid excuse. Instead you can agree goals and measurable targets that relate to the company goals, because a PR campaign in itself is never simply about generating press coverage, it's instead about changing people's minds and/ or influencing their behavior, which can both be measured. Don't accept vague client goals such as "we want to create a buzz" or "we'd like to make an impact." However hungry you are for the business, my advice is never accept a vague brief.

An example of a very clear brief I had from a PR client in the past was: "We want to be at number two in the Google rankings for the search term 'car insurance,' and we want the campaign to appeal to drivers in the UK, especially women." I love a brief like this. It's so simple, I can even remember it years on without looking it up. It was clear when we had achieved the goal and I was able to respond to the brief with a creative solution, for client sign-off. Even better, the client collaborated with me so that they enhanced the media relations campaign with a social media and video content campaign, working across PR, marketing and the SEO team. We hit our goal and won awards. The clarity of the brief they gave me was the key, before I even got to the creative stage. I love clients like this, and you will too.

On the flipside, I have heard of creatives accepting vague briefs such as "I want you to draw me some summer flowers" and then when the artwork comes back, it turns out those weren't the exact summer flowers the client had in mind. I've been as guilty of giving vague briefs over the years as I have of accepting them. But now a warning alarm rings for me and I tend to revisit the vague brief (whether I am the client or the consultant on the project) and discuss tightening it up.

What incentive is there for others working with you to meet these goals too?

Rushing around because you are on a deadline, ignoring other client work, neglecting your family and friends and burning yourself out, to then find that your client doesn't even pay you on time . . . This is a story I hear all too often in the freelance world and it is such a painful one.

To avoid this sad scenario, let's look at how to prevent this happening in the first place. How do we make it our client's incentive as well as ours to meet the deadlines and hit the goals along with us, resulting in happy clients who pay on time?

- Find out what makes them tick . . . what motivates them in their work, and how can the goals and rewards tap into that?
- Make the meetings enjoyable so that your client looks forward to the status meetings and check-ins, and remembers them. If it's not a chore, then they are more likely to tune in.
- Be realistic about what else is happening in your client's world and see if/how you can adapt to accommodate that (within reason). This includes changes that happen halfway through a project, where you may need to revisit and adjust your plans. Allow for open conversations to happen.
- Talk to them about what they will get out of it when the goals are hit. Will it help them get that promotion? Will it pave the way toward an award, or will it simply give them personal satisfaction? What's truly important to them and why should they care? Listen to the answer and, if necessary, and appropriate, change your approach in response.

Finding others who you can celebrate with when things go well can really help too—both for accountability and recognition. Your cheer-leaders for your work might be different people from the ones you celebrate your birthday with, and that's OK.

CHAPTER 4

Unleash your creativity

Tune in to your senses

If I want people to think creatively with me, then I try to encourage them to use all of their senses. Taste and smell are so often left out of our creative thinking for some reason, as we tend to focus on what we see and hear. Leaving out these vital senses can be a huge mistake as they can stimulate feelings of nostalgia, joy, romance, indulgence, pleasure, adventure, warmth or comfort, just to mention a few. If you're brave, you can even use taste and smell to induce disgust! I remember judging a national award where one winning PR campaign featured edible insects on the menu to promote a pest control business.

Sharing food when I want to connect with people and feel at my most creative is incredibly important to me. Humans and animals tend to share food as a way of bonding with our family, loved ones and others in our community. For me, it's a combination of the act of making/serving and sharing of the food as well as the communal nature of the meal itself. The nutritional value of food can help stimulate our brains too.

It's no coincidence that I gravitate toward food-orientated venues for the events I run. People are simply more likely to turn up to your event if it's at a lovely venue. And your brand is inextricably connected to where you opt to meet people as much as your color palette and logo.

Choose to meet people in places that might help them think creatively with you and that offer a positive memorable experience. I've found sponsorship a successful route to funding the catering and venue at my events in the past, from the likes of banks and other providers of business services. I recently attended an event about money and business at a vineyard. I admit 50 percent of the reason I got up early and drove for more than an hour to hear experts talk about finance was the location and view. I learned a lot and met some amazing businesswomen.

It's been traditional for a long time to serve caffeine and sugar or alcohol at events to keep participants wired, but if you actually think a bit about it, it might be better to stimulate people's senses and their minds through vitamins and zingy flavors, rather than stodge and coffee. I'm actually a huge fan of stodge and coffee but bringing Wimbledon-style strawberries and cream into a summer event for a client, with patio doors thrown open on a hot summer day, felt a lot more elegant to me, and seemed to add a real freshness to the evening.

Serving food provides a chance to mingle and network. I've certainly met influential individuals in food queues who I might not have got to speak to otherwise, and had amazing conversations, one-to-one, over a lunch at a conference or festival with interesting introverts who weren't running around broadcasting themselves. I remember having a plate of mac and cheese with a fascinating female brewery owner at a festival and an amazing conversation with a national TV news presenter while lining up for a sandwich at a conference.

Julie Bell is the General Manager at The Felin Fach Griffin in Mid-Wales, a family-run business, which you can find in the Michelin Guide. Julie and I talked about our shared love of food and its role in connecting people, plus our approach to food as creative business women. She says:

> Food is a way that we connect on many levels as humans, from family get-togethers to the memories that certain smells and dishes can evoke. How many times do you walk into a bar at Christmas with the intention of having one type of drink, but smell mulling spices and immediately revert to a mulled wine for its comforting feeling? Good food smells such as baked bread and coffee have, as we know, been used for years as a tactic for selling homes.
>
> In my line of work, hospitality, we regularly see the connections between smells, food and the flow of creative thoughts. A chef is only stimulated in a situation where they have good products, such as the smell of fresh fish coming in, the smell of the first harvest of strawberries still warm off the bushes, the smell of freshly picked herbs. This is why places with the ethos to be able to process these types of food have menus that are a bit

different—they keep the flavours simple, don't overcomplicate the dishes, they aim to stimulate the mouth and therefore the brain. We want the meal to be enjoyed from beginning to end, we look at how the toilets smell, what the soaps are like so your hand washing doesn't impair your olfactory senses. In fact these senses are more important even than the background music. A good meal should mean you don't hear what's happening in the background, there should be enough stimulus on your palate to make this the overriding sense.

Good food and creating an environment to enjoy it is so important to our mental wellbeing. Being creative needs us to be mentally relaxed and in a good place; sharing this eating place with people who feel the same can help stimulate this but most importantly we need to do this for ourselves as we are responsible for our own creativity. We need to look after it by feeding it good food, good smells, good flavors, eating seasonally. Our bodies have not evolved at the same rate as the fast food, convenience food scene and this we can see leads to a myriad of issues. We need to look after our mind as much as our body and I believe that this is why food is such a fundamental part of our being human."

Equip yourself to be at your most creative

Equipping yourself can cover everything from stationery and software to nutrition and natural light. This for me is the most fun part of working for yourself. When I hear of and see clients working in gloomy spare rooms surrounded by piles of washing or discarded items, we might have a chat about why they choose that space. Of course space can be a luxury, which not everyone has at home, but even if your place is tiny, there are things you might wish to consider to improve your working environment. The color of the walls or the pictures you look at every day might affect how you feel about your work. The light might be important, whether it is about sitting near a window with a view or investing in a lamp that emulates natural daylight. For me, an important and inexpensive investment was to buy a small platform for my laptop and an external keyboard and mouse, so that I'm not hunched over when I'm writing. You'll find that you know what you need to thrive and, in general, I tend to hear that the investments are not huge in terms of the money, but there is a little time needed to, perhaps, clear the space or create a routine. In general, just some thinking about what might be missing will help us to find an answer. Repeat this exercise every six months or so if you can—if not every month—as you might find the bad habits creep back in and you're working next to a pile of washing again!

What gets you out of bed?

The answer to this question can reveal the real crux and focus of your business. For you to be at your most creative, we need to tune in to your passion and what drives you.

You might hear people in business talk about your *why* or ask you "what is your why?"

This is why do you do what you do, why is it important and why is it important now.

And perhaps those questions make you feel uncomfortable. If you are an artist and you have always felt compelled to paint or draw, maybe you've never had to look at your *why*—perhaps the answer is just "well, it's what I do." The same may apply to writers. And also a lot of people might answer that they do what they do in order to avoid doing some other thing that they didn't enjoy. So another answer I get a lot is "well I do this because I really hated what I did before." And in that case, let's look at flipping it around and explore what you are working toward rather than what you are running away from.

Perhaps you draw or paint because you are compelled to, but you do this because it allows you freedom. The *why* might be the lifestyle, the ability to say *no* to projects that do not fit with your ethics, or because it enables you to express yourself. It can be any number of things but knowing your *why* will put you in a strong position. And it will support you when things feel just too difficult. Because the answer to why you do this is really about finding your purpose.

If you're already freelancing or running your own business and want to move yourself from a position of *surviving* to *thriving*, then it's likely you're going to need to make some changes. Not simply to boost business but also to be the most creative version of yourself.

And change is rarely easy, so let's make it a little more palatable with some examples:

Changes that might seem out of reach:

1. Moving countries (e.g., if your client base is not in the country you operate from)
2. Entering into a business partnership to grow your business
3. Going back to college, to skill-up

Now these might all seem like extremely drastic actions to take, in order to get the clients you want, but think about how these might be achievable without even leaving the comfort of your own bedroom:

Changes that may feel more achievable:

1. Working remotely with clients in a different time zone, via video calls and other online tools
2. Being part of a virtual collective, teaming up for bigger projects and scaling back for smaller ones
3. Joining an online course, to learn and collaborate from wherever you prefer to work

The idea of these examples is to illustrate that there is more than one way to get to any goal, and ruling out the immediately obvious scary option might prevent us from getting to the goal via another route. Percolate on your available options before throwing any of them out. And don't disregard the big, scary goals, but do explore the baby steps too.

Starting up for the first time can be exhilarating. Everyone likes a launch, with popping corks and freshly printed business cards, the business owner (that's you!) hungry for clients—ready to meet for coffee and keen to offer an introductory discount and new ideas.

I'd recommend making your actual launch (whether it involves a party or is purely online) as being the middle of the first three to six months, not the actual beginning. So I'd suggest the first three months of your business are just about getting a few client projects under your belt, relatively quietly, working out what you stand for and how you like to work, making some mistakes quietly and learning from them. Then after three months, by all means go public and have a bit of fun. This may sound frustrating—because, let's face it, who doesn't want cake and champagne on day one? But I would always advise taking this soft launch approach. Unless you truly believe the *only* way, you can possibly get clients is by having a big public celebration. You know in your heart that isn't the only way to win business, and in my experience, people don't generally win business from launch parties. They win it from doing really great work and being recommended by the people they did really great work for to other people who are in the market for some really great work. The party is a celebration, and some validation for you.

Now, let's explore how to maintain forward momentum once you've begun freelance or small business journey.

- *Routine*: A lot of people new to freelancing struggle with structure, so implementing even a loose structure to your days, weeks and months could be very valuable, especially at the start. When we don't have clients to punctuate our schedule, we have to create our own structure. I still like to do this even in the busy times, so—for example—I have a call every Wednesday morning at 8 a.m. with another freelance friend. And we always have the same theme—money! We know each other well enough to ask each other honestly whether we are on track to make enough that week or month, and to ask each other whether we have too much or too little work, and if that work is stimulating us. It's a really refreshing mid-week check-in, and I do tend to find it most useful when I least feel like having it (when I think I'm too busy to need it or the opposite . . . when I think I'm not doing well enough to justify having a whole call about money as talking about its scarcity can feel fairly icky too).
- *A plan:* At the very start, writing a plan might be on your to-do list and then as you do start to get client work, that pitch and fulfilling the work may eat up all your time, as everything takes longer to start with, and so the plan itself might fall to the bottom of the list. Try not to beat yourself up about it; it's better to have a simple plan written on a

whiteboard than to have no plan because you haven't got around to completing something worthy of a multinational. If you are just one person starting out, have a loose, fluid plan, focusing on what you need instead of no plan at all.

- *A calendar or diary:* While this may sound incredibly obvious, start putting meetings in your calendar, even at the start when perhaps you only have one meeting a week. And make use of the alert options online so that you get a reminder the day before. As well as the obvious reasons why this is a good idea, I tend to find it's incredibly useful to look back at when a meeting took place and have a record of it. Relying on your brain to be a filing system isn't wise.

- *Accountability:* Having a few people in your life to help you stay accountable can be incredibly important and valuable. For some of us, we are the sort of people who respond well to praise and encouragement and so this checking-in is going to work, especially well for us. There can be a sense, when you start working for yourself, of operating in a sort of vacuum, especially if you are setting your own targets and deadlines. Checking-in with someone who has your best interests at heart, whether that's a professional or a like-minded friend, can really help. And when I say like-minded, I'd suggest they are not too like-minded, just that they are interested in what you are trying to achieve. Bringing different personality types into your orbit can be terrific for motivation and offering a different perspective.

Even seasoned, award-winning professionals find it hard to bring momentum every day and experience highs and lows. New Yorker, George Farmer told me:

I've been a freelance musician for over 20 years. Highs have been touring all over the world, winning several Tony awards with several Broadway shows and a Grammy award. The only low, as such, is the ever-present need to hustle for yourself, on your own with very little support.

And when things get tough, George told me his approach is to put even more effort in, and try harder:

> *But that can mean going inward: meditate, relax, accept the present and acknowledge it, for the most part it does mean practise more, with added focus, though.*

We talked about what advice he'd give to other freelancers who are going out on their own for the first time. He says the secret lies in finding your passion:

> *Find what you like and explore that interest to its fullest potential. Sounds easy, but it requires a good understanding of yourself and an honest look at yourself. I find it very helpful to figure out what your likes and dislikes are early on. That necessitates to have an open mind and open heart to really listen to what your self is telling you.*

And the biggest challenge for him is the self-reflection around his art. He says, for him, it's:

> *Constant re-examining of my product/abilities. Constant practise, constant room for improvement.*

A personal project, or passion, can be the catalyst for reaching new heights in your career. Writer and podcaster Lindsay Goldwert was interested in how to get what you want at work. She'd moved from journalism into PR and was not feeling fulfilled in either worlds. So she used her reporting, writing and analytical skills to explore an unusual and completely different world that requires self-motivation, discipline, confidence and excellent communication skills and boundaries. She explored the world of dominatrixes and wrote a book about it. While writing *Bow Down*, Lindsay explored many of the characteristics and elements that successful people in creative, independent careers need to thrive, through the lens of kink and dominance, and while this may raise a few (well-groomed) eyebrows, her journey not only uncovered some invaluable insights, it also led her on a journey of self-discovery and reflection.

Forging your own path as an independent creative person is not about reaching a destination and sitting there with your perfect business cards, big desk and passive income stream, however lovely that might sound . . . Every step in the journey is important and part of who we are and what we do. There isn't really a destination. Even if we are building a company to sell, there's still the question of what happens after that and how we continue to fulfill our true potential and purpose. So if you can find a way to enjoy the process of getting there (wherever *there* might be), then you're onto a winner.

Plans and dreams

It may feel very odd as a sole practitioner to write a business plan. However, without the structure of an office, different departments and colleagues, having a plan is more, not less, important. Without a plan, the focus of your business can easily be blown off course by what your clients want, which can result in not knowing what you stand for, how much you charge or what is around the next corner.

Working from a template will help—I like to use the Prince's Trust template (a UK charity that happens to provide a free business plan template online). There will be plenty of templates to choose from provided by banks, charities and start-up organizations.

If you struggle to create a plan alone, then work with another freelancer. And if you don't know any other freelancers, why not join an online group? There are thousands of other freelancers out there who would love to meet you, compare notes and support you—and you can offer to reciprocate or pay it forward. (I'm not talking about working for free here, this is instead about coffee chats or checking-in.)

Having a plan can help you in a very concrete way—it may help when you're applying for finance (a lender or investor may ask to see the plan) as well as being a guide in itself. Making sure the plan is useful and active is one of the big challenges, especially for a solo practitioner. Ways to make sure the plan stays alive and current can include:

- Pinning the plan up on the wall so that it is visually there for you
- Working through updates on the plan each month with a mentor, coach or other supportive individual

- Journaling, and updating on your plan in your business journal—if you don't like writing, this can be done in any medium you like, from video blog to sketchbook, whatever works for you
- An annual review with your accountant to look at and reflect on your financial progress and financial goals

Your plan should focus on the ultimate desired outcome(s), not simply on the business targets. So for example, you may set a goal of moving to the coast in five years. In order to achieve that, you may decide to set a business target of doubling your turnover, but let's keep in mind that the actual goal is the enjoyment of living by the sea, rather than the larger bank balance. It isn't that we want to underestimate the security and satisfaction of the financial goal—it's more about looking forward to seeing where we are going in our journey and how money is a way to achieve our goals.

CHAPTER 5

Learn and grow

The importance of nourishing your mind as a founder

I spoke again to psychologist and coach Eszter Iván. We discussed how to maintain good mental health as a creative person, especially for those of us who work by ourselves a lot. She says:

I think that what is really important—I can't emphasize this enough—is self-care. When we're passionate about something and really creative, then we can immerse ourselves and really identify completely with it. This can be really good, but if for example there are obstacles, or someone doesn't react the way we'd expect, then we can take it personally. I think then it's really good to be able to find our way and create balance in how we think about it, to really be able to see how the other person sees the world and how they think. We are still valid and still valuable in what we do, but we have to find a way to create a bridge. How can we communicate with them about what we do?

Sometimes I feel that I can be so passionate about my work and about what I do, but for some people it is so alien, something that they never need or they don't know even. If we can know that the person with this other perspective is not against us, but instead take it as an opportunity to express what we do and reach out more and more. I think this kind of mindset can help us to avoid those ups and downs. When this happens we can be more like a witness and observe what's going on, acknowledge it.

I asked Eszter if we should try to look outside of ourselves as an independent observer of our own emotions?

Yes, but I think we cannot be independent. Try to be an observer and see what's happening: go back and acknowledge and see and witness and embrace it. You still have the emotions and you're still living them but this way you process them. I think what I tend to forget and it's good to remind myself—and I would do that with others—is that we are creative people and actually this is our passion and we can use this for ourselves, it's part of the process.

I love what Eszter's saying here, namely that we're resourceful, and we can use that creativity to ask ourselves: "What do I need? What would feel good right now? What's going on here and what's another way of thinking about it?"

She agreed but explained that she has colleagues who work with art, and for them, it doesn't always feel good to use their art to process their emotions:

They say the art for them is different, they're not going to use it for self-care and processing, so they are looking for other approaches. And this is what I find with dancers too: some of them are open to using dance and movement creatively and connecting with their body wisdom, but some of them really want to do something else, explore something else maybe be more verbal or use other art forms, so it's based on individuals, but I think it's about being open, curious and ready to use our creativity.

Working from home, being a *solopreneur* or leading a small team can feel isolating, lonely and pressurized. The support network set up by companies such as HR, team meetings and line managers might feel like something we're glad we left behind when we go freelance, but having no structure might leave you feeling untethered and unsupported. Part of thriving as a creative freelancer is working out how to maintain a healthy mindset and what works for you. Some starting points could be:

- Creating a routine with good boundaries around your availability
- Building exercise/health/wellbeing into your working pattern

- Investing in a coach/therapist/mentor to support you
- Recognizing signs of stress and knowing when to do something about it
- Identifying ways to build your resilience and doing that work
- Having a formal or informal agreement with one or more other freelancer(s)/small businesses to support each other when the workload gets too much or becomes too lean.
- Knowing what helps you personally when you are really up against it—and putting aside time and money for that: whether it's the gym, spa days, regular weekend breaks or something else
- Creating a working environment that you love to be in
- Finding a way to separate home from work—even if that simply looks like clearing your laptop off the kitchen table at 5 p.m.!

Routine and support structures can help keep you well, but if you know that your mental health is a struggle you may need a more robust plan.

Sophie Eggleton is someone who regularly writes, vlogs and talks about maintaining good mental health. She is open in sharing what helps her to thrive in her freelance career as an online creative and presenter, who's currently training in mental health.

Sophie explained that noticing causes of stress was the first step for her:

I decided to really take notice of what was stressing me out day-to-day. Once I had a list I could see any patterns (that I considered whether I might want to stop in their tracks) and decide which things on the list I could realistically do something about quickly and easily.

Sometimes you think it's just the big and obvious things that are causing you stress, and you miss the fact there are lots of small moments that can pile up extra layers on that heap, and tip you over the edge. Sometimes working on reducing, improving or completely eradicating those things can make the bigger things much easier to cope with.

Sophie told me if, for example, she has a lot of filming to do, then she re-organizes her day to create a schedule with fewer interruptions, helping her to be calmer. While this may sound obvious, the reality might involve quite a lot of preparation: saying no to people, planning ahead and perhaps doing less than we originally planned, but the rewards are huge.

The second point Sophie made really resonates with me, as a coach and in terms of my own mental health. She explained a truth so vital, yet one that most of us forget every day. What works for you does not work for everyone and vice versa. If you've ever found yourself telling someone else that they should meditate, try yoga, drink more water or listen to calm music, stop and ask them what they need and what works for them. For example, the worst thing you can do for me if I'm stressed and upset is leave me alone, whereas for some, that is all they need. Sophie explains:

> We can all blog about what relaxes us, calms our anxiety, maintains our mental health, and we share it with good intentions, but that's just it . . . we're talking about what helps us, not what helps you. I know many people find cooking extremely therapeutic for example, but for me it has the exact opposite effect and I turn into angry Gordon Ramsay rather than joyful Ainsley Harriott. So I urge you to make a concerted effort to discover things that genuinely work for you, and not just mindlessly adopt things you've been told are helpful.

Sophie has carved out a wonderful career that sees her meeting and interviewing celebs. I was especially envious and impressed the day she went shoe-shopping with Sarah Jessica Parker! Keeping in mind that we are all human is one of her top tips for staying calm and cool even when face-to-face with your idols:

> Remember everyone is human. I've stressed myself out so many times worrying what people will think if I mess up. If I do something wrong. If I don't perform perfectly. I'm thinking primarily about interviews I've done with artists on days I've felt ill, or struggling with brain fog. There's been times when I've gone blank and lost my way—frantic and panicked in my head trying to find the right words. But when-

ever it's happened, the celebrity/artist has been incredibly kind and seemed kind of unfazed by it. One even placed their hand on mine and said 'don't be silly it's fine, it happens to me all the time'. It's always been a bit of a 'so what?' moment. In fact on most occasions this very human and relatable moment has brought the interviewee and I closer. I think vulnerability and moments that prove we are human and not robots can be what connects us all on a deeper level.

Working for yourself can mean a lot of time at home, especially if your partner is a creative and maybe even works with you too. Sophie's advice on this is to be honest when you know you're having a bad day:

Things can feel a bit tense and claustrophobic in a small flat and you feel constantly on the cusp of an argument. If I know I'm having a wobbly day or wake up with that sense of doom I often get ahead of 'one of those days' I just vocalise it, very plainly. I let Si (my partner) know that I might be a bit short and that I'm a bit on the edge today. It just makes you feel a bit more relaxed that perhaps they won't push your buttons as much as they may have, that they might tread a bit more gently, and that you won't feel as riddled with guilt should you snap unfairly.

Sophie describes herself as an introvert—and I think it's worth making a clear distinction here, between introverted and shy. Sophie is confident in front of a camera and can hold her own, but she also likes to spend time alone. It might be easy to make assumptions about what recharges someone's batteries and assume that if our freelance friends are struggling, that being with others is the answer. Not always so. Once you know what it is that you need to feel better, then bringing that to yourself when things are a bit tough can be vital.

I've worked out that it's not just a preference, I genuinely need time on my own. At times both my partner Si and I have responded in offence when the other has slunk off for alone time, like it's a personal thing and a declaration that the novelty of our company has worn off. We've worked out now that we find the separation less of a statement about our feelings towards each other if we vocalize what we're doing and why. I'll say I'm going next door to watch (insert Netflix show Si isn't interested in) and Si will escape to the lounge for a good session of Call of Duty. Introverts particularly need this time to reset and recharge so it's really important you make it happen.

Routine and goals can really help a lot of us to manage our mental health and Sophie reminded me of this:

Starting a week with realistic and achievable goals has helped me in terms of motivation, but also in terms of giving me a visual (a tick on the list) that allows me to see I am achieving things (however small). It's always OK to be all about the small victories. It also helps to give your week some structure. I find my anxiety worsens without some kind of routine, even if it's a flexible routine—as long as it's one that works for you.

Sophie also points out the importance of being mindful about the content we consume. It's something we have control of and the first step might be to notice how we feel when we come into contact with different types of content, for example on our social media feeds. Sophie describes how she handles it:

I mute or decide to swiftly scroll past those accounts I don't think will serve me well that day. I would say put your phone down entirely, but I understand that's not always realistic for everyone. If you're finding the news a surefire way to ramp up your anxiety, take a break—you can always ask someone to fill you in on all the major points you need to know, or decide to seek it out when you feel mentally more robust.

Freelancing might make us feel more like we need to be everyone's friend than ever before, after all, you never know who is going to be the source of a lucrative referral. But if we are already prone to say yes to everyone, then that might go into overdrive when we're trying to build up a freelance career. Sophie has learned that trying to be everyone's mate is not only not possible, it can also negatively affect our mental health too. She explains:

> *You can't be everyone's friend. This has been a long and arduous lesson to learn but boy, do I feel liberated now I've really applied that concept. Because we can be connected to so many people now (due to social media) it doesn't mean we should or that it's beneficial to do so. I used to try so hard to maintain my place in so many friendship groups I ran myself ragged by either trying to be in too many places in person or keep up with the dross in WhatsApp group chats. Ultimately I never felt a core member of any of the groups because I was spreading myself thinly, and never quite able to keep up. I also wasn't enjoying the connections, as my overworked self meant that they started to feel like a chore and a pressure. So in the last year or so I've let some friendships naturally fizzle. I figured if I didn't hear from them as I eased my efforts perhaps the drift was meant to be or that it's just the way the friendship is meant to be at least (as less intense/ sporadic one). I know now I'm much happier with just a few friends. It feels more manageable and I don't end up feeling like a failure all the time for not managing to be at another birthday party or social event.*

While hibernation and disconnecting a little might recharge the batteries of an introvert, reaching out to others in the same boat can be soothing for many of us, introverts and extroverts alike at different times. Luckily, there are plenty of online and in-person networks to support people who want to find their squad.

Jenny Stallard set up a network for freelancers in March 2019. She wasn't happy freelancing but knew she wanted to carry on working for herself even though work was scarce and, like many of us, she was at home on her own. Her partner works from home too but was sometimes at meetings and Jenny felt hugely isolated. She found plenty of support for the *how* of freelancing—groups and sites—but not so much about the *why* and what she perfectly describes as *the feels*.

> *I always wanted to be freelance—I set up Freelance Feels to almost stop me going back to a staff job ever! But I know it's always going to be hard. I think the key thing we need to do is understand that, and work with it rather than against it. I've spent a lot of my life trying to be 'more normal' and 'less angry'. The more I sit with those things and just say 'I'm me' and find clients and a way of life that fits with my mental health, the better (and more powerful) I feel.*

> *I would urge anyone who is struggling to reach out to other freelancers for help, via groups or meet ups. Be honest about how you're feeling. If things are really bad talk to your doctor or a charity like Samaritans USA.*

> *If you can, share highs and lows with your family—I did, with my sister, and she encouraged me to set up Freelance Feels. It's credit to her, in part, that I'm now speaking as the founder to you!*

The idea for *Freelance Feels* began when Jenny wanted to explore her own feelings about her career, and she realized her default way to do this is by writing. So she began to plot a blog. Once she had chosen the name, *Freelance Feels*, her blog began to take shape.

Turning to social media was next for Jenny—she started an Instagram account and interest in her blog built up. Then she set a launch date, which, she says, was terrifying! But Jenny says:

> *If I wanted to do this, to create something, I had to see how it went, plus, I wanted others to know they weren't alone in the feels. That it's OK to have crap freelance days and to lament this choice we make. To feel a failure and rubbish about it one day and delighted the next. To create a squad that felt honest and open.*

Obviously, good mental health is vital for all workers, not just freelancers, but I was keen to find out what Jenny thinks the unique challenges of freelancing are, especially when it comes to mental health and wellbeing in general. She explains:

> *Isolation, finances, marketing yourself and having to be everything from the admin to the social media to the cleaner! You have to hustle for and secure your own work, make your books balance and be your own IT, HR and wellbeing departments. It's exhausting and all that isn't even your job! That's on top of your job! Training? That's your department! Pay rise? Up to you . . . it's all consuming and that can't help but have an impact on mental health.*

> *As freelancers we have, often, flexible time but we can get sucked into working and not taking holiday, to not exercising and to eating badly. Finances have a huge, if not the biggest, impact on freelance mental health. For me they are the baseline of our wellbeing. Having a buffer helps, setting rates and so on, but that all then makes us feel everything from nervous to unworthy.*

Some freelancers like the flexibility of being able to work around the ebb and flow of their mental health or other health conditions and find the flexibility allows them to manage it. I wondered if Jenny has found that in her network and what insights it's brought? I suspect the *traditional* workplace could learn a lot from freelancing.

> *It's very varied. I do and always have done a lot of in-house shifts which are a double-edged sword, as they bring routine and you know what you're up to, but then you can't be so flexible! I've found they help my mental health because they give me routine and money on a certain day but they can damage it as you're always the new girl and that's mentally draining. I've heard others speak about how it's great to be able to hide away at home and still work. I've certainly had days like that.*

> *I so agree that the trad workplace could learn a lot from freelancing— so many now have people working from home, essentially freelancing in a way, but with no support to manage that change. They also have a lot of freelancers in-house who, with the best will in the world, get*

left out, forgotten (such as when they go for lunch) or treated like a glorified intern!

Flexibility means I can fit in things that are good for my mental health—exercise, dog walking (I borrow from friends) and eating well—or better, at least.

I also asked Jenny if there are any trends she's seen—or would like to predict—when it comes to freelancing for creative people?

Coworking seems to be on the rise and I don't see that stopping. I think meet-ups will be more prevalent and also mentoring. I see more people mentoring and one podcast interviewee says he co-mentors with a friend.

We're used to being guarded as freelancers, protecting our clients and so on, but I think collaboration and sharing, will be more prevalent. And being more open about the fact it's not all roses!

In 2019, social media company Buffer's report: 'The State of Remote Work'[1] explored the views of 2,500 remote workers. The study revealed that loneliness (19 percent) and unplugging after work (20 percent) were the two biggest struggles with working remotely. Commenting on the findings, Amir Salihefendic, CEO of Doist, explained: "We need to acknowledge that isolation, anxiety, and depression are significant problems when working remotely, and we must figure out ways and systems to resolve these complex issues."

Combatting imposter syndrome

You may have experienced, or heard of, the concept of imposter syndrome. It's the sense that "somebody will find me out, and when they do, well they won't want to hire me anymore," (or date me anymore, or whatever the context might be). It's the idea of not being *good enough* to be in your role or do what you do. And what's made this a hell of a lot worse in my view has been decades of people going around suggesting we

---

[1] https://buffer.com/state-of-remote-work-2019

should "fake it till we make it," which I disagree with so strongly, it makes me feel a little unwell when I hear that phrase!

If you are having one of those days where you're feeling like a fraud and your confidence is plummeting, there are plenty of ways to combat imposter syndrome without faking it:

- Be yourself
- Find out what it is you really like about yourself
- Focus on doing the stuff you really love, and doing it as well as you possibly can
- Market yourself in an authentic and bold way that works for you
- Ask others, who you respect and trust, what they really like about you

My problem with the "fake it till you make it" mantra, is the idea that you have to be something other than your real self. In fact, I believe the opposite is true. The solution is to be the most yourself that you can be.

If you're in a workplace that wants to mold you into a sausage and that sausage doesn't fit your idea of who you truly are, I suspect there is always going to be a conflict, at least internally within you, between the sausage and the real you. And that sounds to me like an incredibly stressful way to live. But the more you fake it to make it, then you start becoming a bit you and a bit sausage and then it might even be hard to tell who you are and feel easier to become 100 percent sausage and not at all you. Which might even mean you end up faking your former self when you go back to your hometown for Christmas. And you know what, if you are happy being transformed into a corporate sausage and that fits with your goals and ambitions, I'm not suggesting that in itself is bad. What is bad for me is the idea of someone so anxious and so uncomfortable in themselves and in the version of themselves they are projecting that they actually feel sick when they cross the road to the office, like a subverted Pavlov's dog, an involuntary reaction that predicts when something bad is coming. And if that thing that you don't want to arrive is your day at work, and you don't feel like the person that they are expecting, pretending to be that person is going to get exhausting. In fact, it might make you ill.

The great news is that I do have an antidote. An antidote to imposter syndrome and to the uncomfortable feeling of not belonging.

Being yourself. Two little words with a whole lot of meaning behind them. The trouble might be that we've been faking it for so long we no longer remember who we are or what we like. In that case, let's turn for support to someone who knows exactly who they are and has been being themselves and forging their own path successfully for decades.

Fiona Chow runs Goadi Consulting Limited in Manchester, UK, and prior to that worked in senior roles at well-known PR agencies in London. Being authentic is part of how she operates and people who work with her know what they are signing up for. She is unapologetic about her personality and her lack of ambiguity is incredibly refreshing!

As a communications expert specializing in work with startups in consumer technology, advertising and marketing technology and professional services, she works around the world and with people who handle eye-watering amounts of money for a living. She's also a marketing advisor or director to a number of ICO (Initial Coin Offering) and blockchain clients, which she says is often considered a bit like the Wild West, a role not for the faint hearted or sedentary.

Authenticity is key to how Fiona operates—giving her clients honest and thoughtful guidance, without pulling any punches. She explains:

> *I think the concept of work-life balance is almost as outdated as Robert Owen's 200-year-old "Eight hours work, eight hours rest, eight hours leisure" model. As a single working mum, the thought of eight hours rest or leisure is pretty laughable!*
>
> *I prefer the concept of a work-life blend, which doesn't assume you're on a factory clock-in, clock out routine, or in fact, that you're some kind of automaton that is only ever either at work, or at life. The best kind of work and the best kind of life interact in harmony to enhance the other aspect.*

The thing about Fiona's work-life blend is that she's not putting herself under a ton of pressure to jump in and out of different personas and roles the whole time. Yes, of course she might speak slightly differently to her son Max, than to a CEO client (well, perhaps, it depends on the situation!) but essentially by not bowing to the corporate idea that we all have to be a different person at work and at home she's making life a little easier for herself and playing to her strengths at the same time. There are a lot of things I admire in Fiona, and one of those is her incredible consistency. The Jekyll and Hyde characters of some PRs I've worked with in the past have literally been like a character walking off the set of a play or TV show and totally changing the moment they loosen their tie or kick off their heels. While that might work really well for some people, Fiona's approach to a work-life blend has worked in her favor and her clients' favor too. She says:

You can only do this effectively if you are authentic, honest and able to set boundaries in the right places - less of a border wall, but a running stream that bends and flows with the landscape but nonetheless has a clear objective and goal in mind. The journey towards that goal has to be enjoyed and enjoyable and that means being true to yourself.

This manifests itself in the type of clients I work with and choose to cultivate. These are generally entrepreneurial in mindset, focused on output rather than admin, straight-talking and fast-acting. They prefer plain speaking, debate rather than dictate and value those with values. This then gives me the freedom to be my best self: nurturer, cheerleader, champion and conscience.

Someone once said I gave "zero f**ks". That is not true, I'm all f**ks : f**k this, f**k that, f**k it, f**k you!

When entering into discussions with a prospect I am internally marking them against three pillars of happiness and asking "Will working with this person make me a) happy b) rich or c) famous?" I insist on a minimum of two out of three, with potential to bring happiness scoring the highest if in doubt. I have to credit the amazing Angie Moxham, founder of 3 Monkeys Communications and now founder and Chief Angel at the Fourth Angel and my best ever boss for that philosophy. She also inspired the name of my company, as she once said that the thing she liked best about me was my "Get On And Do It" approach (hence GOADI).

Conversations with clients have to be peer-to-peer, both operating as subject matter experts and respecting what the other has to offer. Relationships have to be built on mutual respect. Without that, I can't operate at my best.

And she's taken this blend even further by taking her son Max on an overseas business trip and holding the client meeting at the Science Museum there, while Max ran riot around the interactive displays.

For me, there are several benefits to occasionally taking this approach:

- The meeting is going to be more fun for everyone
- Her son gets to see Mum as a great role model
- She's signaling to the client that she is creative and resourceful and able to simultaneously prioritize the most important people in her life in an incredibly charming way

And everyone gets a story out of it too. Fiona posted photos of her day out on social media, with her client's permission, and it served as a beautiful case study of her authentic approach. I know Fiona, and I know she wasn't pulling a stunt—this is who she is, genuine and upfront.

When your new business isn't new and shiny anymore . . .

So what do you do when you're a year in, or 10 years in, and that initial hunger and energy has dissipated?

One of the reasons people tell me they go freelance is to never have to walk into a toxic office again. However, freelancing does not always free us from the tyranny of tricky clients or the struggle of making ends meet. In fact, unpaid invoices and angry customers can be harder to handle on your own as it can feel personal and the consequences can be more immediate and impactful than in a larger organization. And this can be draining.

So if you get to Sunday night and think "I don't want to go to work tomorrow," then some action and care is needed. Staying in bed on

Monday morning is the last resort and not one I'd advocate unless you are contagiously unwell!

How to fall back in love
with your creative career

I'm going to offer you some practical techniques for moving forward and maintaining motivation and energy:

Take a working vacation

For me, taking my laptop to the Spanish coast when it's raining in my home of Wales tends to bring a new life to my work. Writing my journal outside a cafe in a tiny cobbled Spanish street, while eating delicious fresh bread and tomatoes with olive oil makes it hard to hate my job, and the flights are incredibly inexpensive. I appreciate this isn't great for the carbon footprint, but any way of getting a new perspective is valid here.

Do a job swap or simply visit another business

I spent my 40th birthday visiting a gin distillery that makes cheese and a chocolate factory that serves cocktails. Seeing how other businesses work, and having a slice of birthday cake with them, is a lovely way to celebrate and hearing other people talk passionately about why they love working for themselves reminded me of why I love working for myself and with other entrepreneurs.

Have a hiatus and then come back to it

Freelance and founder life isn't something that the door ever shuts on... Unless you've gone to jail or gone very badly bankrupt, you can walk out and back into freelance life again. I do not think it does any harm and in fact might do some good. I went to work in a brewery for a year shortly after I lost two very close friends: one to cancer and one to a heart attack. I was finding it incredibly hard to get out of bed in the mornings to run my own thing and so I decided to spend 12 months putting my energy into something that a younger, more energetic person had created. I left my house at 6.15 a.m. every morning and drove around 40 miles each way, every weekday for a year. I often cried on the long drive for my friends who I missed. And in between the crying and driving, I worked my ass off, both physically and mentally. I learned new skills, developed fresh networks and did jobs and tasks I had certainly never done before or never expected to do. Running a beer festival for the first time for someone with very little beer knowledge and poor spatial awareness is a learning curve, to put it mildly. And at the end of the year, I found the strength to go back to running my own thing, with a new approach and some different ideas.

An appetite to learn

Learning can quickly go out of the window when a freelancer realizes that they might have to pay for it themselves. It can feel like a double-whammy because a lot of training courses and events are not priced well for the solo practitioner and that day out of the office means you are not earning in the traditional sense of the word. Investing in your self-development is vital, though. Especially at the start.

From a small-ish business decision such as what software to use, right up to whether a business owner or freelancer should take investment, research and learning will almost always enhance the ability of the decision-maker to see and think clearly and make the best decision they can at the time.

The great news is that there are thriving, friendly communities of freelancers online and in cities and towns across the world. I have met thousands of freelancers over the years—online and in person—and I've never met one who didn't wish to support other freelancers who are asking thoughtful questions and showing an appetite to learn.

Learning and continuous professional development can really enable you to thrive as a creative freelancer. It's easy to know this and not take any action though. Why? Because learning new things is hard! We are set in our ways, we are used to our old or current ways of thinking, our current thought processes and learned patterns and behavior. Learning can take us outside of our comfort zones, challenge us, ask us to think in new ways and spend time with new ideas. We may have really unpleasant memories from school or college that we associate with learning, which make it feel like something we don't really want to do. And then there's creating time for it—even if we do budget the cash, then we know that there is a whole lot of reading and thinking, which will have to happen to make it worthwhile. It all sounds rather exhausting, perhaps! So I like to think of it this way. . .

Learning can help to bring a feeling of legitimacy to your work—whether you learn as part of an industry body, an informal or formal network or an academic institution, it can help to set you apart from your competitors and, for some of us, it may help us feel more professional. We'll also develop new ideas and new ways of working through our learning. These could save us time, help us earn more money, open doors for us and plenty more. It can bring us connection as we meet other experts through our learning—even if we're studying remotely and connect with them online. And it can feel rewarding—learning can bring us a feeling of fulfilment and personal growth. In fact, once we have that appetite for it learning becomes part of our DNA—perhaps it already is part of your routine. In summary, learning can:

- *Offer you new qualifications*: While this may seem obvious and not all creative skills are connected to passing exams, having a certificate from an industry body can help build trust and encourage best practice, both for your own practice and for your clients.
- *Keep you current*: If you are guiding your clients, they will want to know it is with the latest knowledge and not with something you learned a decade ago that may have been superseded by now.
- *Enhance and expand your networks*: Whether you're attending a one-day seminar or embarking on a diploma or degree, you'll no doubt meet clients and potential clients while you are learning, as well as possible collaborators. Your peers can be an amazing source of support, and where better to meet them than on a course to hone your skills in your chosen niche

Sharon Wheeler is a senior lecturer in journalism and PR at the University of the West of England, UK. She explains:

The best investment you can make in your career is to keep learning. In a fast-moving field like the media and PR, skills and knowledge can grow stale very quickly. If you don't adapt, you won't survive! You can certainly pay for various professional qualifications or post-graduate courses, but these tend to be serious money. So look around for workshops or e-courses that might be more affordable. Networking events are great for chatting to people and finding out how they've topped up their skills over the years. If you belong to a professional body or a trade union, take advantage of subsidised courses. And never look on learning as a chore—it makes you employable!

Photographer Paul Clarke agrees that learning is vital as a solo creative and also that, in general, we tend to be very bad at it as a group! He says:

Solo creative types generally undertrain themselves—it's a mixture of things and legitimately there's some time pressure. If you have a busy diary with client work as I've had, then giving up a day a month or two days a month to learning something is not insignificant.

There's a fear thing—why would I want to learn something different? I'm very comfortable with the skill-set I've got.

So there are reasons why we undertrain, but I would say generally we do undertrain ourselves, and there are probably some good reasons for it, but it doesn't alter that fact.

As Paul notices, there is a connection between learning and being outside of our comfort zones—admitting we don't know everything, preparing to be wrong and/or to fail as we learn. And so when we think about the combination of giving up time, investing money and being open to making mistakes, learning can sound incredibly daunting. It also separates those who become true experts and stay current from those who become stuck. Stuck at a certain ability level or stuck with how much they can potentially earn. And part of that could be that if we do teach ourselves a different process or approach, then it might change the way we do things fundamentally. Once we have evaluated the old way and new approach, we might decide that the way we've always done things is no longer the most useful. And that can shake us as perhaps we discover that we need to change the approach we've based our whole business on.

Listening—to yourself and others

Listening to your clients, interrogating the brief and really hearing their feedback can make you a great practitioner. Listening to yourself—trusting your instincts and tuning in to your gut instinct—will also stand you in good stead. If you have a chemistry meeting with a potential client and something feels a bit off or not quite right, then try to tune in to that, see what it's telling you and what you need to learn from it. Freelancers will often know in advance which clients are going to be tricky, who will not pay on time and who is not a good fit, but can feel drawn to sign up the wrong fit client based on the idea that it's better to have the work or money than an empty schedule. While there's always a balance to strike, between having enough money to put food on the table and turning down clients who aren't the right fit, then having a plan and a strategy can help you out of that feast or famine cycle.

Listening to what your clients want, and what's getting in their way, can help you really begin to develop an understanding of *your* role in the process. Don't be afraid to reflect back what you think you heard in order to clarify the brief, and also put it in writing to check that you have understood it correctly. Asking more questions—especially *why?*—and also speaking to other members of the team, customers and stakeholders, can be useful for larger tasks and projects.

Listening to, and tuning into, what your clients want and need is a skill to practice and hone over time. Learning to really listen well, and ask insightful questions, grows with practice and can help turn your freelance career or agency from simply actioning client requests and being a spare pair of hands, into becoming a trusted and wise consultant and expert. Books such as *Time To Think* by Nancy Kline can help you understand how to become a better listener.

A lot of creative freelancers complain that they are hired to *action* and *do* rather than think or consult. If you are in the position of being hired as a *do-er* and you want to be hired as a thinker and a strategist, then reflect on how you communicate with your client and whether you could change that. You might need to change who you talk or listen to as well as how you communicate with them. Find out what they really want to achieve, both individually and strategically, and think about how you can help them to get there. Making assumptions about what you think they want and/or being a *yes* person and not challenging them could stand in the way between being a do-er and a thinker. If you want to consult rather than temp, your relationship with your client may need to alter or grow up.

Growing your team

If you begin as a freelancer or company of one, then growth might initially look like taking on board other freelancers on a project basis, and at some point, you might win a big contract or grow in such a way as you take on a team member. You've probably been building your brand and reputation around yourself as an individual and so taking on your first team member can feel huge, even if to the outside world it might look like quite subtle growth. To you, it may feel nerve-wracking, and suddenly, you are responsible not only for someone else's success but also their mistakes too! I turned to photographer Paul Clarke to find out how he managed growing his event photography business and learn from mistakes, which were not always his own, but his team's too:

> I think my starting point on this is that you absolutely can't have a sustainable team if you're going to behave in a way which relies on fear. But there was a really bad one a few years ago. It was a very inexperienced photographer who was technically very very good but didn't really understand what needed to happen in the shoot.
>
> It turned out that they shot the entire event other than the full audience shot—now the client then comes screaming 'Where's the full audience shot? It's the one that we want to market it with.'

We had 1,200 people in the room and there's no single picture of them all. And they hadn't done it—it was a mistake and it obviously wasn't fixable because I couldn't then go and get 1,200 people.

What are my options there? Make them feel like they never want to shoot again? Get really prescriptive and write down shot lists? Or the approach that I took, which was to say 'I will deal with the fallout from this.'

So I carried it all and I offered the guy an entire event shoot for free for one missing shot. He didn't accept it, and I think I ended up discounting the fees . . . I basically overcompensated, but it was the best thing I thought I could do.

But for the photographer, I said let's go back to some basics. So before you even pick up the camera, why have they [the client] got us there—let's do the mindset thing. What are they trying to show?

And what this photographer was really good at was [taking] absolutely amazingly beautiful pictures, but they were often people on their own in the corridors in beautiful light working or thinking or whatever.

So [the wrong message we'd be giving with these shots would be] 'ok come to this event where you'll be on your own' and yeah, it's a great picture but it's absolutely not what the client can use.

The education process had to almost set aside the technicality of what we were doing and just think about the motivation—why have they hired us here: 'Popularity, interaction, collaboration, diversity.' That's your brief—start with that.

What Paul had to then say to the photographer, who was part of his team, was:

I know your comfort zone is to make the most beautiful picture you can with the light and setting available, and do loads of those, but honestly you could have sent me 2000 beautiful pictures of people on iPhones in lonely long corridors with amazing converging lines and I'd have spiked every single one.

So that's the business question for us as creative consultants: 'Why am I here?' 'What does success look like?'

You need to have a conversation like that . . . and that went well and they've become incredibly trustworthy. But my approach has always been that you can't throw blame around—there's no point, is there. If there is a good reason why it should have been different, teach the reason, don't teach the mistake. Teach the reason not the action. And that's my advice on that.

CHAPTER 6

Attract new clients

Leaving the relative safety and security of your day job to set up on your own may be driven by a desire for more freedom, creativity, flexibility and the chance to really realize your potential. For your clients, you're there to solve a problem for them—their goal is not generally to boost your business, but to boost their own. With that in mind, think about the problem you can solve, and who you want to solve it for.

Research your target audience

For me, immersing myself in the world of the client has always been my chosen way of connecting. If I wanted to understand more about how to sell kung-fu classes or bottles of wine, I'd attend a kung-fu class and a wine fair. Yes these are both real examples, and I had the bruises to show from, err . . . both experiences. (Drink responsibly, folks!)

There are an unlimited number of ways to research your target market. I usually choose the ones that I find fun and which involve eating or drinking, but I am told that reading research reports can be valuable too. Here are some ways to get under the skin of your chosen market:

- Holding focus groups
- Reading articles, trade publications and specialist media
- Reading research reports: your client's, their competitors and industry reports
- Conducting your own research
- Attending conferences and events within the field or industry
- Learning and development: courses and experiences
- Interviewing specialists and experts
- Back to the floor—spend a day (or more) working in your chosen field at the coal face

The mistake a lot of people make with new business is they think that there is a work persona and a business persona, and when they have their suit on and a name badge, and they're drinking lukewarm coffee in a conference center that they are driving new business, but that when they are sitting reading a magazine or newspaper supplement on a Sunday morning, they are not driving new business. However, if that magazine has a regular column that features businesses like yours or your clients', and you choose to go and follow that journalist or editor on Twitter and respond with a really relevant insight or case study when they need it, you might find yourself making a lot more sales. As that article hits thousands of eyeballs than you will reach more customers or clients than you would have done by chatting over lukewarm coffee in a conference center to a bunch of people who are also there to drive new business. I don't mean don't go to the conference, but keep your eyes open to opportunities all around you and follow the ones that resonate and feel authentic and natural to you.

Actions you can take to help drive new business for yourself:

- **Map out who you know**
  Your network is bigger than you realize! By mapping out who you know, you'll be likely to notice opportunities and connections, which you may not have thought of before: create a diagram, such as a bubble chart, of who you know, and who they know. Remind yourself of your networks, and set yourself some realistic targets around contacting them over the coming weeks and months. Keep a record of who you got in touch with and how it went. Do something every day toward this goal if you can—even just five minutes per day can be enough time to reconnect with a contact on LinkedIn or arrange a coffee catch-up with a former colleague. Reflect on it every month to see how your network is growing and spend some time thinking about how your business expertise could be the answer to their problems. How you then take those relationships forward is key—it could be offering a free consultation; supporting a charity event they are running or more blatantly asking how your expertise might be able to drive their business forward. Your instincts will serve you well in knowing how to approach each person in your network to boost your business and help theirs to thrive too.

- **Get social**

  Spending a day (at least) going over your social media connections, especially paying attention to business-focused connections, and reaching out to people you'd like to reconnect with. Keep a note of who you've reached out to, and make sure your own profile reflects the type of work you'd like to attract. Investing time in keeping your own profiles fresh and current is an important part of this—check that your bio says clearly and plainly what you do and how people can get hold of you. While spam e-mails can be irritating, making it easy for your clients and potential clients to contact you is more important than the seconds it takes to remove spam messages from your inbox. If you are reaching out to people but making it hard to get to you, you may be putting up barriers to new business. Don't hide behind an online form—instead provide an e-mail address on your social profiles.

- **Celebrate and share past successes**

  Reflect on the best work you've done so far in your career—what would you like to be known for and how can you remind people that you're great at it? Gathering client testimonials and recommendations can be reassuring as well as great for business. Instead of taking your word for it, having others recommend you can be a great way to drive new business enquiries, plus it can be a welcome confidence boost for solo workers to be reminded of how brilliant you are!

  If you work in a role where you can show specific changes and improvement and quantify them, then that can look powerful in your case studies too—whether it's money raised or saved, or footfall increased. If your clients are happy for you to shout about exactly how much you boosted their business by, then do use those figures to promote your expertise.

- **Explore what people think you're brilliant at**

  Ask people close to you what you're great at—you may be surprised to hear what they say. This could provide clues to what services or packages or products you offer as well as how you describe what you do. It's possible that what clients really love about your work is not the main thing you promote. Consider creating new or enhanced versions of the services you offer—you may want to trial and develop them before rolling them out widely, perhaps trial them with a smaller or niche audience first.

Market yourself

The main mistake that freelancers make when it comes to marketing is to only think about it when they need money or new business. But marketing is always best carried out consistently and continuously, rather than in peaks and troughs. It is not a tool to be used in desperation—not least as that desperation is likely to show. If you doubt this, then think about some of the biggest and most successful brands in the world. And think about how consistently, loudly and proudly they continue to market themselves over years and decades of success. Being busy is not a useful reason for putting the brakes on promoting yourself.

If you're committed—for example—to sharing updates on social media every day, but you've chosen a platform that really doesn't tap in to what you enjoy, then you've set yourself up for failure. It might sound obvious, but I hear people every day asking me how they can populate their Instagram when they are not fond of taking or being in photos or what role their blog will play when they do not have a writing habit. Listen to yourself and make your passion the center of your marketing strategy. Communicate in a way that feels natural and fun.

Even if you love it, finding the time to market your expertise when you're at your busiest is a serious challenge. Lurching from intensely busy periods of client work to a feeling of tumbleweed and—perhaps—a sudden panic around where your next wage is coming from, can be very unsettling. And while we know this, then justifying the time, money and energy needed to market your business when business is thriving—only to turn clients away—can feel like a huge waste of time.

So how can we manage to market ourselves when we're really up against it?

- Use the quiet time to set things up in advance, making it very easy to keep marketing momentum up when we're at our busiest: whether it's batch-creating social media content and imagery or pre-planning a series of adverts for the next six months, using the quiet times fruitfully can be very rewarding.

- Create a process for handling new business enquiries at busy times. This could involve outsourcing (the client management and/or the marketing); creating waiting lists; working with other businesses or any number of innovative approaches. Research how other businesses manage this and see what might work for you.

- Having a marketing plan to follow, alongside your business plan, which will help you create a steady, sustainable flow of potential new business. The aim is to be able to choose the clients you want, not just take everything that comes along. This approach will allow you to be in the driving seat, running your operation, rather than feeling like an employee of your most demanding clients.

Having an abundance of potential clients or customers knocking on the door not only allows you the freedom to choose who you want to work with, but you can also decide how much you'd like to charge and when you'd like to work. Being able to schedule projects in for the rest of the year is a godsend if you can stomach the initial chaos of marketing yourself when you are at your absolute busiest.

To get to that point of abundance may take several years of establishing and building your brand, reputation and offering. There are so many different ways to promote yourself, I'd recommend expending most energy on the tactics that feel authentic to you.

Tactics that can help you build up your visibility and reputation include:

- Hosting and/or guesting on a podcast
  - This can help in a number of ways. As well as improving your brand awareness, your guests will become part of your expanding network and you will learn and practise different skills as you create the episodes.

- Writing a regular newsletter or blog
  - Try not to think of it as marketing—make it useful and practical for your audience
  - Share it via a number of different platforms and cross-promote it
  - Commit to it for at least a year—and don't be discouraged if the first few get little traction—it will gather momentum over time
- Regular and consistent social media posting: focusing on a few key themes
  - Choose a social platform that works for you, you don't have to be everything to everyone. Practise with a few different platforms before committing to one, and when you do commit aim to post at least once a week. Batch creation of content and/or a content strategy can really help. If you find it outside of your comfort zone, then call in professional support to help you create that. Whether it's words or images you need help with, there will always be someone who can support you.
- Speaking at business events
  - This may sound terrifying, and/or time-consuming to some, but second-nature to others of us. Before you write it off, consider that business events come in all shapes and sizes. Your ideal event could involve you speaking to an audience at a festival sitting on hay bales and enjoying a beverage—it's not essential for speaking slots to involve a conference center and smart suit if that's not your thing. And if conference centers are your thing, that's perfectly OK too! Find your authentic place and make that the starting point for your speaking tour.
- Charity volunteering, using your professional skills
  - While protecting your income is vital and *no free work* can be an important boundary, volunteering for a cause you love can be empowering. As well as helping you connect with like-minded individuals, think of it as your corporate social responsibility and a chance to put community at the heart of your business.

- Sitting on the board of an organization that you are passionate about
  - Similar to charity volunteering, sitting as a non-executive on a board or fundraising committee can help to flex new muscles and network you with different groups. It's often enjoyable and of course you're helping a good cause in the process. It's also a chance to stretch outside of your chosen sector or embed yourself more firmly within it.
- Using another skill to complement your main business—so for example you may be a strategist who also offers facilitation, and this can help build your reputation
  - Working out what your secondary skill is might surprise you. As mentioned previously, if you don't immediately know what it is, try asking your friends, clients and former colleagues what they think you're great at. I'm often asked to provide content strategies for social media, even though I don't recall ever promoting this as a service I provide. I've been approached to write CVs, bios, content plans and strategies because those people who approached me thought they liked the way I did mine and wanted a similar vibe. So don't underestimate what you are naturally good at—you'll have skills that come very easily to you and because they are easy to you doesn't mean they're not incredibly valuable to others. Clearly some professions require certification but not all do—experience and passion are important factors.
- Cross-promoting your skills and expertise with trusted people in your network—for example, a recruiter and a career coach may work together—can be cost-effective and add an extra layer of support and accountability. You can either have a formal or reciprocal agreement or a more relaxed approach to cross-promotion. Some people will charge or pay a fee for referrals; personally I prefer to suggest good freelancers and consultants who I am proud to recommend, not because there is a fee there for me.

- Writing a guest column or posts in a trade publication or regional publication or relevant blog
  - This visibility can raise your profile in areas and networks beyond those you know personally and help to support your portfolio or bio or CV too
- Contributing expert comments to journalists for business articles, books and other publications (such as research reports or white papers)
  - Identifying these opportunities yourself could be done on social media or through networking, or you might choose to recruit a PR expert to support you. I'd advise quality over quantity, choose a few key publications that are consumed by your target audience, rather than taking a scattergun approach or going for everything that comes along
- Adopting an unusual or groundbreaking way of working and sharing the results
  - This can open up your creative valves and give you permission to think more laterally. Either notice something that you already do differently or identify a new way of working that is congruent with your brand and eye-catching in some way. For example, as part of my own self-care, I like to go swimming at least once a week, which feels fairly normal and unremarkable. In the summer months, I do my swimming in the river, which to some is exciting or brave. To folks who live where I live, it is our normality and a visit to the river is as common in July and August as a trip to the shops. It's where you bump into all your friends and chat or gossip or catch-up. Once I realized that swimming in the river was not normal to all my online followers, I'd occasionally post about it, and it created a whole new conversational thread and group of followers. I'm not saying you need to jump in the river where you live, just look at what in your life is part of you and also remarkable to some. Where those two points meet could be a happy place for social posting.
- Focusing on your values and beliefs and living or breathing that publicly—whether it's veganism or a passion for

architecture, can help you to find clients who share your values and beliefs as well as drawing attention to your passion and expertise

- Your passions and beliefs are the essence of you and of your personal brand, identifying them and gravitating toward them will create the authenticity that so many strive for and can fail to hit. Fake authenticity can feel so cynical and to create it for real can involve a certain element of vulnerability. Think about how much of yourself you are prepared to share and what you want or need to keep back for yourself.

- Highlighting a hobby or pastime that complements your consultancy work. You might be a mindfulness expert who loves to create pottery or a graphic designer who also enjoys life drawing. Sharing this can help you to find and expand your squad as well as being a conversation-starter

  - Whatever brings you joy is likely to be shared by others too . . . and is, hopefully, enjoyable to write or photograph or share too, making your task a little easier

- Telling your story… not the PR story that is glossy and polished, but the real you. This could be something deeply personal or very light and amusing. It's important to stay within your boundaries and only share as much as you want to, but these touch-points can really help people to see the real you and add a genuinely authentic tone to your communications.

  - This could be sharing your journey as a carer or parent or volunteer or something similar. As long as you are keeping yourself and those close to you safe in terms of how much detail you share, it can feel empowering and gives a more real sense of who you are, with depth and a humanness.

When considering your marketing strategy, a great starting point is to ask yourself what you would like people to think, feel or do as a result of interacting with your communications. Think about appealing to their senses. People absorb information in different ways and so relying on one form of communication can mean you unwittingly cut out a host of potential clients. For example, you might be a visual person and yet many of your potential clients could be audio people who'd love to hear your voice on a podcast or radio show, on the phone or at a presentation. Think laterally about how to include as many of the senses as possible into your marketing and promotions, as you will also increase how much people recall about your brand if they are able to immerse themselves in it.

It's easy for your marketing to begin with good intentions and then drop off, so having an accountability buddy can help immensely. Choose someone you can be honest with, who you can trust to keep confidentiality and who you are happy to be challenged by. You may find that this works reciprocally between you or that you perform this role for someone else, not the same person who does this for you. Either way, choose at least one person to help keep you accountable as driving your marketing forward on your own can feel a little thankless at times!

An effective marketing strategy does not have to cost money. But if you have no budget to invest in your marketing, you will need to have at least one or more of these other important ingredients:

- *Time:* To market yourself effectively takes time and patience over a sustained period, ideally you'll work on it every day.
- *Inspiration:* As a creative person, you may feel like all of your creativity goes outward into your clients' work and there's nothing left for you at the end of the day. If this is the case, then I'd urge you to carve out time and space to focus on crafting and implementing your own marketing plan. It may feel tricky to start with as it's not chargeable time, but I promise you'll get a return on investment from it.
- *A clear message:* Knowing what you stand for and what you would like your audience to think; feel or do as a result of interacting with your marketing is central here. Create your message, and test it. Change behavior or change how people think. Make them feel something, experience a particular emotion. Make them care. You may find your messaging evolves over time.

A perfect example of a marketing approach that is incredibly effective, almost free to implement and very inspiring, is the social media account of *Addyman Books*. This happens to be run on Instagram (find the account at: @addymanbooks), and yet really, it could be operated on almost any platform as long as the same approach and consistency was applied.

Anne Brichto who is co-owner of *Addyman Books*, and runs their online account, looks after three bookshops with her business partner and their small team. In fact, not just three bookshops but three *magical* bookshops. This is not only the description of her business in her online bio but also how most fans of *Addyman's* would describe their experience too. Now let's put this in context. Hay-on-Wye is a town with a population of approximately 1,500 people[1]. And yet, more than 6,000 people have *liked* a photo of Anne's bed, and in excess of 65,000 people have seen it. It's a nice enough bed, with a packed bookshelf running alongside it, in the eaves of an old building, but what makes this photo so *likeable* in a social media sense is its context. Anne has built a brand for her shop and for her social media account, in the context of the *brand* of Hay itself. The town itself is a branding masterpiece, and Anne's business is one of its strongest exports, perhaps second only to the festival itself.

Hay was a sleepy market town on the English/Welsh borders—I mean it still is—but something changed. In the 1960s, a wonderfully eccentric entrepreneur, Richard Booth, saw an opportunity. He had noticed that libraries were closing down and began importing books from closed-down libraries into Hay from the United States. The town became a town of books and of bookshops and publicity stunts such as Richard Booth crowning himself the *King of Hay* and declaring the town an independent kingdom, in the 1970s. The town of books began its own literary festival in the 1980s and so this town gradually grew in reputation and with a consistent theme of second-hand books, became a focus for bibliophiles not just in the UK but also worldwide. An estimated 80,000 people visit the festival each year, with a total of half a million estimated to visit this tiny town itself annually. And remember that this is a town with a population of 1,500!

---

[1] *source: www.hay-on-wye.co.uk*

Anne is still slightly astonished at the public's appetite for a behind-the-scenes look inside her bookshops and home: "6,000 people have now liked my bed and 64,000 people have seen it. The world is a very strange place," she says.

Here's how Anne of *Addyman's* carves her niche and sustains her brand through Instagram:

- Anne works with and not against her competitors, with initiatives such as Hay's *Bookstagram* and other activities that involve her fellow booksellers. This is a community, not a competition.
- She makes her feed personal, authentic and consistent, with themes that run again and again, which people know to expect and enjoy engaging with.
- She makes her fans, and fans of the town, incredibly welcome and engages with them, online and in real life, hosting annual breakfast events.
- Anne makes her posts look very natural in their beauty, and it is not entirely obvious that she actually takes hours creating her beautifully themed *booksellers' breakfast* posts, often sacrificing her actual breakfast so that we can enjoy looking at a beautifully coordinated smoothie that perfectly complements the covers of the theme's books and vase of flowers: behind-the-scenes of these stunning food and book combinations are a sinkful of cold, congealed smoothies and cold teas or coffees.
- She combines her passion for books with a passion and talent for visual displays, food and community and is also a great photographer, using her camera phone to its fullest potential.
- And she keeps it consistent and relevant. Each post also features books from her shop, which are for sale—it is a sales tool but you'd be forgiven for thinking that she is doing us a favor by posting it. And, well she is, filling our worlds with literature, insight and personal stories that she tags generously to connect to other small businesses and readers or fans alike.

I asked Anne about how she developed her online account, and we talked a little about how it has been a lifeline for her during the time the shop was closed for months during 2020, because of the coronavirus pandemic. She explained to me that she started on a different platform—Twitter—and for some reason, it didn't quite gel with her. These weren't her people and she came off it deciding that social media just wasn't her thing, going back quickly to her analogue world. But she was open to listening to her grown-up children and taking their advice on how to get the next generation engaged in reading and buying second-hand books and her son, Thorne, suggested Instagram. Now this is another thing that Anne got right from the get-go. She noticed that if one social media platform wasn't for her, it didn't mean she shouldn't try out another one. Trying and failing is an important part of building a creative career or business, and being resilient enough to try another platform was an important part of building this brand. And without meaning to cast aspersions, there is also perhaps some bravery in starting a social media account in your 50s, going slightly against the grain as 59 percent of the platform's users' average age is between 18 and 29 and 90 percent are under 35 years old. Which is actually perfect, as bringing this age group on board as fans of the book town, as fans of physical, tangible second-hand books and of this tiny chain of magical bookstores is more important than engaging their parents and grandparents. This is the generation of Audible, Amazon and Tik Tok. And surely enough, Anne's following of more than 30,000 has an average age demographic of 25–34 and are mainly in the UK and United States, as well as followers around the world.

What is lovely about her approach is how unselfconscious it is. The commentary, which is long-form by Instagram standards, contains a mixture of very personal updates such as what was cooked and eaten for dinner and who it was eaten with in the lovely flat above the bookshop itself, to the more ethereal, historic and literary. Imagery and themes of seabirds, marbled pages, Alice-in-Wonderland and first editions sit comfortably with updates from the local market, the local vicar with his giant poodles and talented next-door-neighbor who creates beautiful visual art. Anne is a wise and thoughtful person and observes cleverly but not without opinion and openness. And this is the magical mixture that sustains her online world and sees it growing and increasing in popularity. This is combined with the time she invests in personally commenting and replying not just visibly online for several hours a day but also in private messages and e-mails, of which she receives 100 or more per day. Somehow she also manages to volunteer at least once a week at a helpline for children and achieve a number of other incredible roles in her work and life, all with a mischievous smile!

Build and establish your brand

Identify the essence of your business and what sets it apart when you're pitching for new clients. This may come down to how you are—be it super-creative, inspiring and full of energy or calm, cool in a crisis and experienced. Whatever your *unique selling point* (USP), it has to be the answer to someone else's problem. Remember to make it about your customer, not about you. They need to know what's in it for them and why they should care.

Your USP could be based around a method or system that is unique to you, or you may offer a service that many others also offer, but you are the only one doing that thing in your town. Whatever it is, being able to describe it in a few words—sometimes known as your elevator pitch[2], will help you market yourself and feel more confident. If you don't yet have an elevator pitch, then enjoy creating one. It can be a lot of fun. And don't underestimate how long it can take to create a short, snappy sentence! It might take you a year or more to come up with an elevator pitch that you are entirely happy with. And then it may evolve and change as your business evolves.

Once you've researched and established what it is you stand for and the message you want to communicate to prospective customers, you have permission to do the fun part, namely establishing your brand.

Zoë Doyle, who's a creative director and works with influential brands such as Estée Lauder, Unilever and Marks and Spencer, explains

---

[2] This is based on the idea that one day you might meet that influential investor or decision-maker in an elevator and have the duration of the ride to pitch your idea to them.

how freelancers and small businesses can embrace a strong brand without forking out thousands. She says:

A strong brand presence can be achieved very simply but takes thought and planning. The key is consistency, you want to be consistent and considered in your branding so it's quickly recognizable. Once you have developed your initial branding with, say, logos and a colour palette, stick to and apply this to all that you do. This includes things like what you are wearing in terms of colours and patterns in your instagram posts. Everything you do should always be checkpointed back to your branding key document to see if it falls in line. If it doesn't, don't post it! Yes, good engagement and content is key but it's also very simple to keep it visually on brand. Most people when they find your website or social media will decide within five seconds if they want to look further. If it is a mess and doesn't look cohesive you will lose their attention before they get the chance to delve deeper.

Zoë's tips on effective branding:

- Invest your money in an experienced graphic designer or branding company to set the tone of brand for your business. You may think good design is expensive, but I promise you done badly it's more expensive as you will limit your business from growing due to looking non-professional, and customers might not have the same confidence in you. You don't have to look corporate to do this, just considered and consistent.
- Set up your brand color palette along with any other branding like logos first thing once you know the direction of your business. Make sure you are totally happy with it, then go forth in sticking to this throughout all communications for a clear brand business message.
- Always review social media from a bigger picture. Look at your home page grid, does your profile picture encapsulate your branding ethos? Are you wearing a bright pink T-shirt on

holiday as it's the only photo you like of yourself but all your branding colorways are neutral and earth toned? This sends a message to your customer that you are not confident in your message. It's easy now to set up your own mini portrait shoot with the timer setting on your phone camera. Wear an outfit in line with your branding and take your time to get a photo you want to use for the long run.

- Typography is as important to carry through as any image and color theory to your marketing. Make sure you have all fonts from your designer so that you can have cohesive typography. It's always a red flag if I see different styles of font being used across a brand that don't work together. You may think they look sort of the same, but it's not good enough, it's so easy to keep them the same and look like you have used a designer to create everything. The best thing to do is also ask for a web equivalent font for things like newsletters if you are going to go forth in creating your own content after using a designer for the initial brand work.

- If you don't have design programs like Adobe Suite, there is a website called Canva, which is great and can be used with some practice. However, it is always better to use an experienced designer where budget allows but have a go and see how close you can get using your own hands, if for no other reason than it being fun!

If this all sounds a bit daunting, you might want to return to it when the time feels right. Zoë has been an incredibly patient friend to me when I made the time and space to really focus on my own brand, and I don't underestimate the power of having a pal like her.

If you're still stuck on your USP, I have an intriguing approach you may wish to try. It involves exploring qualities that you think of as failures or mistakes or flaws, because these could secretly be your super-power! Well, for me, when I first moved to Wales from London, I didn't really tell many people I was here. I used to get up incredibly early in the morning to travel to London for meetings and brush under the carpet the fact I lived in between fields and farms. I saw it as a bit of a drawback not being in the city. But gradually over the years, I realized that living in a historical building in the middle of nowhere, surrounded by myths and legends, poetry, art, music and nature was part of my selling point. I had a different and unusual perspective, which I could bring to the table for my clients. Instead of dressing in a neutral or city way, I realized that my vintage or handmade clothes (not handmade by me but by local businesses) were part of my brand and part of my personality and so instead of adopting a neutrality to fit in when I went to London, I began to bring more of the real me to the table and stopped apologizing for it. Looking back, it sounds obvious, but I think I feared being thought of as *small town* and worried that might lead to losing work. Instead, it had the opposite effect of making me more memorable.

Three examples of how to live your brand:

- You're never seen without your dog, who attends all your clients meetings in dog-friendly cafes.
- You are an early-riser and love working with clients who are early-risers too, you're totally happy to have meetings at 7.30 a.m., and this has helped you find a niche but loyal client base of earlybirds.
- You have a really good understanding of disability needs and specialize in working with clients in the accessibility space— you're passionate about accessibility and this shines through

So many of my clients come to me asking for support finding their niche, and there are a number of questions we can ask ourselves on that exciting journey. Many of us may have followed a path that was not in the original plan, and through promotion or relocation, found ourselves in a role that doesn't entirely fit with what fulfills us, and at the same time, perhaps we do not know what that is.

Discover your niche:

- Think about what you loved doing as a child, at six or seven years old, and what you wanted to be when you grew up.

- What activity allows you to find your flow? What is it that you do that becomes so absorbing that the time just flies and you *lose* yourself in it?
- What fits with your values and beliefs and allows you to feel truly congruent with who you are and what you believe in?
- What would your colleagues over the years say you are really great at? This could be something you are already known for but perhaps does not sit centrally to your role at the moment.
- What would you like to learn more about and enjoy reading or researching in your spare time?
- What elements need to be present in order for you to feel truly happy? If you are only truly at one with yourself when you are outdoors or with animals, but you have a desk job, you might want to rethink your niche!

Using your vulnerabilities and uniqueness as an asset

The adage about making lemonade when life gives you lemons is overused, but there is something in the idea of turning adversity into sweetness. The same could be said of using your perceived weaknesses or extreme obstacles you have faced or are facing as assets and opportunities in your freelance business. Let's look at some examples:

Natalie Trice spent so much time in hospital appointments with her son, who was born with a rare condition, that she ended up creating a powerful community and writing a book about it, which she successfully got published. This journey through adversity led her to write a second book (on a totally different topic) and so she is now an author as well as a successful freelance consultant with a thriving business. I'll tell her story shortly.

Craig and Aimee who both almost died (one battling cancer, the other breaking their neck) and having both pulled through, they vowed never to have a *normal job* again. I tell their story in more detail in the section on digital nomads.

It's not essential to be facing adversity in order to tune in to your unique talents. Conducting an audit of what makes you different can provide lots of clues to what could make your freelance business different from others and help you to stand apart as well as helping you to work in a way that's congruent with who you are. And of course this may change and evolve over time too. Your core values and skills could be the key to your success—and the way in which you work can also hold clues to the future of your business and how you run it.

For Natalie Trice, freelance life gave her the freedom to relocate and make some powerful changes to her life. She tells me what happened:

"After my son had his seventh operation at age six, and was recovering from having his pelvis broken and remade, I decided things needed to change."

Natalie had been—in her own words—"a party girl with a fab London life." She enjoyed a TV career taking her around the world, a glamorous lifestyle that involved having her own driver and plenty of designer shoes. Switching the Jimmy Choos for flip flops and international travel for walks on the beach in her new home of Devon was a huge gear change for Natalie. This change led her to find better health for herself and her family, and offered her the space and time to write and publish her second book. This time it wasn't a book about her son's illness but a book about her PR expertise—sharing her expert knowledge with other women wanting the same sort of freedom and fulfillment that Natalie has found for herself. Balancing her career, family and relocation was in itself time-consuming, and Natalie has found that scheduling time for herself, and for each task, is essential. She advises:

As a mum as well as a business owner and charity founder, there simply aren't enough hours in the day. You want to be the very best in all elements of your life, but this isn't always possible and if something gives, it is usually your health!

I try to block out time each day to do tasks, including coffee breaks, dog walks and even putting the washing on! Be realistic, because an extra day in the week is never going to happen.

Building your squad

Just because you work on your own does not mean you are alone on your freelance journey—far from it. The freelance community, especially when it comes to creative people, is one of the most supportive and welcoming of any I've encountered. If it feels like you are by yourself, think about who you'd like to be in your *work family*. You might not get it right the first time—allow for your network to grow, settle and alter. You will notice who gives you energy and who sucks it out of you. Respond to that, welcoming in the energy-givers and aiming to spend less time with the energy vampires!

Ways to build your freelance squad

- Joining an industry body or group
  Think laterally about this, it doesn't have to be one of the stuffy ones! It could be a society for people who like whisky or a creative organization. Find something that works for you and try to make your subscription worth the investment by attending some of the events or engaging in the group. If what you are looking for doesn't exist, then consider creating something with a friend.

- Setting up a virtual community, such as a Facebook group
  I did this when I started out as a freelance PR. By the time I handed over the group I'd set up, it had been running for eight years and had attracted 3,000 people who identified themselves as freelance PRs, mostly in the UK. There is at least one conversation happening there every single day, and we created an offshoot group for new business as so many people began to use the group to find work or to find a freelancer. Both groups are thriving, and it helped me to feel supported when I was both new to freelancing and physically isolated living rurally and remotely. It often surprised people to hear that I set up the group because I was lonely! It's now become a place of comfort for others. And how can you be lonely with 3,000 people to talk with every day who get what it's like?

- Networking locally or regionally
Once again, this really does not have to be about dull, faceless, conference rooms. Networking locally could mean embracing what your local area is known for: it could be a food festival, a sight of natural or historical interest, music, art—almost anything that you feel passionate about. Connect and introduce yourself as a small business owner, tell them what you do, find like-minded individuals and connect with them. In my area, we have a social media group that meets at the tapas restaurant in our town once a month. There are drinks and laughs, and we take turns to research and present on a social media platform or idea. A lot of heckling and fun happens and we learn too, but most importantly, we connect with a flexible group of intelligent and creative individuals, and no question is ever too silly! We've had fascinating and in-depth conversations about neuro-diversity and confidence as well as the ins and out of algorithms. It's free and open to anyone in the area.

- Build a map of your network
It may seem funny to draw out on a piece of paper who you know—surely this information is clear to you already? Not necessarily true, as different arms of your map or diagram could open up ideas you haven't thought of. For example, does your bank hold small business events or advice? That friend from university—could they be a potential client? Your cousin who's an accountant—could they support you in some way and/or you them? Map out who you know, and build up your network week-on-week and year-on-year. Keep a track of your connections (and of who you have offered what to!) so that you can see your progress and uphold any promises you might have made or explore opportunities that are open to you.

CHAPTER 7

Choose how you run your business

Alex Myers founded his global PR agency *Manifest* a decade ago. He has offices in London, New York, Stockholm, Manchester and soon to be Melbourne.

He started *Manifest* alone in his living room in London, with no initial investment, and won the world-famous beer company *BrewDog* as a client right at the beginning of his journey.

If there's anyone who knows a thing or two about pitching creatively, winning clients who are a good fit, and holding on to your intellectual property (IP), it's Alex. We sat down to talk about this and got straight into the vital stuff early on. I asked him about the pitching process in PR as I'm aware it's an industry where the expectation is to reveal detailed campaign ideas at the pitch stage. I understand that this traditional model can cause tremendous challenges, especially for smaller agencies looking to make an impact. Alex believes the process is ripe for disruption:

There's no other industry that does give away their IP, and does the work that they're meant to be paid for at the pitch process. It undermines their strategic value from day one. Effectively we're paid for the delivery of ideas which no one's paid for and therefore we're selected as consultants, but paid for like cleaners—just on an hourly rate—and that's how it rolls. So that's one of the main reasons it's broken.

The principle element for an agency to consider, especially a small agency, is how much are you willing to give away?

If you want this work you have to be willing to give up your creative ideas. So you have to want the work because effectively you're giving something in order to receive.

If you're giving away everything to everyone then it feels much more harrowing and I feel like being able to say no to some people and giving what you need to, to the people you're willing to say yes to, at least puts you in a sense of control. It also means you're more likely to win the pitch, which is basically the outcome that everyone wants. The way to win more work is generally to pitch for less of it.

I find Alex's insight here so valuable. There is plenty of advice out there about new business being a numbers game, in that the more you pitch for, the more you win, but *Manifest's* approach turns this right on its head. Alex told me why he advocates being very selective about the work you pitch for:

It's not a numbers game if you're a strategic counsel, it's a numbers game if every pitch you push out is the same thing. What we're talking about here is when there's a creative response, which means you have to consider it. Anyone who works in the creative industries as an 'on demand creative' knows that it's very difficult to just move on to the next creative mindset.

The acknowledgment that creative pitching takes something out of us and is not like a sausage factory is really important here. It's something we need to think about as business owners when we are creating a culture. What are we actually asking of people? If we're looking for real inspiration and powerful ideas, then spreading ourselves too thinly can lead to burnout or simply to sub-standard work. Alex told me it wasn't how they worked at the start, they used to pitch twice a week every week:

As we've grown, the number of pitches we pursue has now reduced and that's a significant learning. A few years in we introduced a client scorecard, because it's really difficult to say no to work. It's easily the hardest lesson to learn. You should be saying no from day one because all that does is add value. There's this idea people have that they'll say no when they're big enough, but it doesn't work that way because you've already created this script that is you, or your agency, saying yes.

If you start out with this mindset, it becomes part of your brand and how your business operates. That selectiveness means you are choosing the kinds of clients you and your brand want to do business with, so it strengthens your operation as well. Alex agrees:

Definitely, we're a purpose-driven business, we have a triple bottom line which means we address everything based on three kinds of profit: financial profit, planetary profit and people profit. We assess the opportunity for a net growth that a brief brings us. Now sometimes it's going to be growth from a people or KPI (Key Performance Indicator) in a sense that our team gets to do something they've never done before. Learning growth is going to have a positive impact on people. If we know the campaign we're going to deliver has a positive message about the planet, around promoting sustainable business practices for example, that scores more highly.

We also have our company values which are the deal breakers on the scorecards, so if anything contradicts any of our company values it's a straight no—it's a one strike you're out basically. I think that that's super important to have. Someone once said to me 'well that must cost you money', and I said 'well, a value's not a value unless it costs you money'. I think a principle is only a principle when it's difficult to pursue. Yesterday there was a conversation at work about a brand that should change its name for various contextual reasons and it was in Australia and it's sort of un-Australian to admit that you're wrong, but it's the right thing to do, and if the right thing to do was easy everyone would just do it and not have a problem with it all of the time.

Alex is at the top of his game in PR agency terms, with a string of awards to his name and his agency's name, but that *imposter syndrome* feeling still affects him, as it does so many of us, and I told him I found this reassuring because it normalizes that emotion for the rest of us! He says:

> We're now ten years in, we're now an international agency of the year two years running and I wake up every morning thinking 'someone's going to find me out today'. I think it was David Ogilvy that said good creatives have 'divine discontent', where there's the constant pursuit of perfection knowing that it can never be there.
>
> My colleagues will always tell me that I say 'what's next?' too quickly, so if we win some amazing work that is a negative because I don't celebrate and validate, which is what everyone wants me to do. But then when we lose work or lose a pitch I'll say: 'all right what's next?' and that's seen as a positive, because I'm moving on quickly and not dwelling on it, and trying to learn from it. I think that naturally comes from the panic of being an owner. It's like you're building something without a sort of end point, so you're constantly saying: 'we can do better, we can do more, we can improve', and also constantly thinking 'I'm not good enough'. But if you channel that in the right way it doesn't become self-hate it becomes a positive, because instead of saying: 'I'm not good enough', it's like saying: 'I can be better today, and get closer to not feeling like this', but it is a constant and it's something that I think you become more comfortable with when you can control it and own it a bit more. I think when I was younger and running the agency, when it was smaller, it was still a positive influence, but I think in the pitch process it definitely made me somewhat of a victim. I would be giving it all and doing it without considering how much value was being given to the pitches that I lost.
>
> I remember one of the first things that made me realize Manifest was a bit different was that we won the pitch for BrewDog against around thirty five agencies and Manifest was just me at the time—it was one of our earliest clients. When I went to meet the co-founder James for the kick-off meeting, he basically said 'oh I'm going to send you all of the thirty five pitch decks so you can pick out any ideas you think will work' and I said 'no you're not'. So something I've found out since,

only very recently, this was about ten years ago, but something I've found out since that is that James shared the winning pitch deck with all the agencies that lost, and said 'yours wasn't as good as this', which I've never heard of before or since. I think it's the kind of thing that if he did that with my knowledge it would have been slightly different.

We ended up parting ways with BrewDog due to IP discussions. Now I think we're much better at protecting that IP, so the thing I would say is the first rule of negotiations is a real cliche— and which is the only thing I'd ever learnt about negotiations—give them what they want on your terms.

Alex's most powerful advice—and something I agree with from my heart—is to really get to know the client's business and make it a partnership you're entering into, not a hierarchical relationship:

Manifest was set up as a business out of a mixture of naivety and bravado! But it was also a demand to have a more direct impact on brands. That simply wasn't available at traditional agencies and if people understand that you get their business objectives and you share their passion to achieve them, that is a partnership.

Don't get me wrong, there's an investment from the agency side that needs to happen, but the pitch is a shallow investment. The investments we made in the early days, which now we still do, is work experience with every client: the whole team. So if it's a retailer then we're working on the tills. I've been on roofs doing roof tiling, I've delivered parcels at 5am in the morning, because you need to understand the brand.

And that approach, which Alex embeds across his business, and now doesn't even think of as a huge part of their proposition, as he takes it for granted, is what differentiates a winning pitch from a mediocre one. That appetite and ability to live the client's brand. And if you don't feel like you want to do that, you are not a great fit. I explained to Alex that I'd done the same, I'd got bruised doing kung-fu with a client (who was a kung-fu master), pulled pints, waited tables and done all sorts of jobs to understand better how to PR a business. And it works. If you only take one piece of advice from this entire book, go and do the grown-up work experience. You won't regret it.

Structure and systems

While structure and systems are actually among the first things you'd ideally put in place, it can feel overwhelming and confusing to try to establish systems before you begin, as you simply don't know what will flow easily and where the struggles exist. However, I'd guard against going too far down the road without any systems—especially the ones that have legal implications!

After the first two weeks of starting your business, set aside a day to review your current ways of working and for setting up some great habits, systems, processes and structure. Some people will love this more than the actual work itself, while to others, it may feel like the most unpleasant day of your working life! However good or bad it feels, you're going to thank yourself once it's done. If it doesn't come naturally to you or feel good, then consider rewarding yourself and/or working with a pal or virtual assistant to support you. Here are some of the sort of systems and structures you may wish to think about. You will have more and/or different tasks depending on the nature of your business and only you know what they are. If in doubt, consult your accountant and/or business advisor for input on what else you might want/need.

Sarah Childs specializes in looking after operations, project management and studio management for creative small businesses and freelancers in Manchester, UK.

I asked her about flexibility and freedom, versus the importance of structure and systems and whether you can have both, or whether the desire to be flexible tends to hold creative people back from implementing structure.

Sarah explained that working for yourself can enable greater flexibility, but this requires the owner to be disciplined. Her work is all about setting up systems and structure, whether that's to support a business that is growing or a one-person operation where processes simply don't exist or perhaps have slipped.

"Having systems and structure in place can increase your productivity. So, it can allow you greater flexibility in a way," she says.

Sarah described to me the importance of establishing a set of core values around how your business operates. She feels that this can help you to be more flexible and can possibly make you more productive with time too.

It may take practice. Sarah advises that discipline is the key, and this can help you to develop successful habits and practices. Not in the sense that everything has to be rigid, but habitual in terms of being daily or monthly, for example. And the whole point of this is to give yourself more time, so by investing a few hours in setting up your new structures and processes, the rewards will be an increase in your productivity, and you will be freer to be more creative as you won't be held back by the (perhaps) more mundane aspects of running a business.

Sarah explains that putting good structure and useful habits in place is part of working on, not just in the business. And her clients then discover that they can be both more productive and more creative in the time they free up.

Sarah recommends creating the following good habits within your business or freelance operation:

- Set yourself a specific time each day or week or month to tackle regular tasks such as receipts, mileage, timesheets, invoices and so on.
- Prioritize the week ahead in advance—either at the end of the week or the start of a new week.
- Identify which part of the day tends to be your most productive time of the day—for many people, this is mid-morning—and schedule the in-depth tasks that really need your concentration during this window.
- Schedule tasks such as admin toward the end of the day so that you free up the middle of the day for the work that takes more concentration.
- Inbox management: keep your inbox as clear as possible. The only e-mails in your inbox should be those that need to

be actioned, and that should be about 8–10 maximum. For the rest, have a well-established folder system, including your clients appearing alphabetically and also have a really good labeling system.

- Be honest in your communications: if you get a quote from a supplier and you know the project isn't going to happen, then give them feedback rather than leaving them hanging—this is just good practice.

- Factor in unpaid internal admin into your planning: if you work, say, 40 hours a week, then not all of those hours are going to be chargeable. When you're starting out, nobody really tells you that. It's good to work out what your base figure is.

- Pick up the phone: sometimes it just saves time, compared to e-mailing.

I made a little confession to Sarah around this point in our conversation, as I was starting to feel a little guilty. I have a perpetual note in my calendar at 8.30 a.m. every day for an hour that says *admin hour*—and I see it and think "ooh interesting words"—and I don't do anything, I just see the words. Since speaking to Sarah, I've organized my life by outsourcing my incomplete admin to a virtual assistant!

Sarah and I also talked about the difference between *out of scope* versus *over and above*. Having managed many creative studios and projects, she's noticed that sometimes creatives will deliver more than what their brief has asked them for, because they want to do the best by the client. And she's also witnessed the opposite side to that where you're not even interested in doing the tweaks or working on a last-minute deadline. She says it's another one of those areas where you might burn your bridges if you don't handle it correctly. For me as a coach, I always talk to my clients about the values and beliefs at the core of their business and also their boundaries. While I would not urge creative freelancers and agencies to be at the beck and call of their clients, I would encourage them to work out how they want to show up and sensing when pulling out all the stops is important. What Sarah says about not burning your bridges is the key here. And if communication starts to break down, then having an honest conversation can set things on the right road again, or, if you need to end the relationship, wind it down in a way that works for everyone.

If you struggle with spreadsheets, as many creative people tell me they do, Sarah suggests using them to create useful diagrams. For example, mapping your clients and your new business pipelines against your potential targets for the month—or getting someone to do that for you. I have to be honest I would not know where to begin but would love help to do this. This can give you great visibility over your work, cash flow and forecasts and even what your team is doing. It helps with planning ahead, and once again supports you on your way toward flexibility and freedom. Sarah says:

> *It doesn't all need to be spreadsheets and it doesn't all need to be scary and I think that there are different things—if some people had demonstrated what spreadsheets might offer them for example a cash-flow forecast—something simple that documents where your clients and your pipelines are against your potential target month. Your targets can then be illustrated to someone in a basic format.*

Processes and systems to consider

- Accountancy or book-keeping
- CRM (customer relationship management)
- Data and IT security
- Filing systems passwording or encrypting
- Synching your phone or laptop or files or software systems
- Contracts for your clients, as well as terms and conditions
- Pricing structure and process for chasing payments
- Content strategy
- Photo or image library
- Branding
- Marketing plan, to include website and business cards or leaflets (printed or virtual)
- Company or business structure (such as limited business or partnership or sole trader)
- Booking system (if relevant)

- Premises: such as a co-working space, meeting room hire, home office
- A structure for feedback and reviewing work
- Logistics: everything from storage of goods to how you plan to get to meetings
- Working day: When are you open for business and what happens to enquiries outside of hours?

I explored these themes further with Annie Browne who runs a virtual assistant business called *Hello My PA* and she's discovered that throwing money at clever and expensive tools often isn't the answer—it's more about working backward from where you want to get to. She explains:

One of the biggest myths around business organisation is that you have to invest large amounts of money. I have had many conversations with small business owners who are considering spending or have already spent a lot of money on a tool that promises to save them time, increase their sales and all manner of other things, only for them to discover that it doesn't provide what they need.

My tip would be to decide exactly what it is you are trying to achieve before you start researching tools and applications, rather than trying to map chaos into a snazzy tool that has been recommended to you. A Client Relationship Management (CRM) system is the first thing I always recommend having in place. Always. A CRM system is not only a way to keep track of potential clients, existing customers and their profiles but many also allow you to organize workflow, connect to your accounts system and collaborate with teams. I have used a free version of one particular CRM since day one and it still serves me four years into the business. I have never paid for a CRM.

As well as being a freelance virtual PA, Annie Browne is also the co-founder and director of *Freelance Heroes*, an online community for UK-based freelancers. Having started her freelance career in 2012 running craft workshops and documenting her crafting journey via a blog,

Annie went on to start her virtual assistant business, *Hello My PA*, in 2015 after having two children. She's a true advocate for the concept of work-life blend, and believes that being freelance opens up a whole world of opportunities when it comes to lifestyle.

Raising her children while looking after many clients across a variety of sectors, managing a small team and running *Freelance Heroes* is no mean feat. Annie explains how she handles this: "It is all about momentum. As long as you are doing something, you are always moving forward."

She's highly organized and intent on making time for herself as a priority, and believes that you are the central cog in your freelance life and you set the pace from the inside out.

PR expert Victoria Moffat learned, by doing, that structure and systems could help her regain the balance she craved in her work/life and also that the investment she made would come back to her in profitability. But it took five years to really get to the point where everything flowed, she reflected that she kept making the same mistakes again and again. It wasn't until she took a step back and gained some perspective that she had a real lightbulb moment. Victoria explains:

> *I started my business in 2012 and in 2013 I got pregnant. My son came along in 2014 in May. Being a first-time Mum I didn't know what it would look like, how it would be. I thought 'I can totally wing this'. I remember writing an award entry when my son was five days old, and thinking 'what have you done Moffatt? And . . . it won!*

While Victoria continued to *wing it*, as she says, for the next five years, working with freelancers and using her expertise as a former lawyer to build up her specialist PR business, she kept getting the feeling that something wasn't quite right and eventually called in an expert, in the form of Sarah Childs, (whose expertise is also quoted earlier in this book). Sarah offers support to MDs, agency owners, established freelancers and independent folk, looking to take their business to the next level.

Sarah helped Victoria work *on*, rather than solely *in* her business.

For five years, Victoria had run her business without creating processes, and it turned out to be an ineffective way to operate. She explains:

So my early attempts at outsourcing was speaking to freelancers and saying 'so this is the client and . . . go!' Just saying 'come on guys, you can do this' so obviously that didn't work for the client, for the freelancers, for me or the business, but I just kept doing it – I did it for about five years, I didn't really know why it wasn't working.

I met with Sarah and said 'This is the situation I find myself in, can you help me? How much is it going to cost? What does your help look like?'

And actually looking back, for her it was like the easiest thing in the world, but for me, the effect of having invested that money on the business: oh my god, I can't tell you how much improved everything is, I've gone from being a blubbering mess, to having this amazing process that works really really well.

I have a fantastic team. The steps which we've actually taken were huge at the time but now it works so well, why did I spend the last few years just saying 'just do this'?

Professional bodies

A lot of qualifications—and awards—that may be relevant for freelancers will be run by professional bodies. And they can also offer a support network. My advice would be to try one, if you don't like it, try another one the following year. What I have learned—like with so many things in life—is you really do get out what you put in. If you join a professional organization and yet you don't make any effort to engage, then of course you're likely to think it's a waste of time.

I'd recommend subscribing to professional bodies and groups that offer assets such as:

- Templates such as contracts—which are legally binding and you can adapt knowing it is endorsed by the industry body you belong to.

- Affordable access to professional services and financial services such as accountants, legal advice and banking—some memberships are worth the subscription solely for this, as it practically pays for itself in terms of the cash you can save.
- Community and networking—a great source of referrals to boost your new business efforts, as well as providing support from like-minded people.
- Awards and learning—whether it's a one-day course or a professional qualification, an annual award for your work or the chance to sit on a judging panel, this can really help you to skill up.
- Space! Some membership bodies have lovely buildings where you can hotdesk or hold meetings or events. In the first year working remotely, I practically lived at the Chartered Institute of Public Relations (CIPR) in London—I discovered that they had, at the time, a members' room with free tea and coffee, rolling news and a reception and cloakroom so I treated it like my own private members' club as it was very sparsely populated.
- Participation—as well as using the members' area I also enjoyed volunteering to run events and became a judge at the annual awards too. (I'm not afraid to own being a *girly swot* when it comes to these things!) While it was time-consuming, the pitches from the shortlisted award entrants were really inspiring and motivating. Plus of course it didn't look bad on my bio or CV either. Committees can be a drag, but the only way to make them more lively is to get involved and put some of your personality into them.
- Fun. Find a professional body that aligns with your brand and your personality and which you enjoy being a part of.

Private members' clubs and co-working

Very much like professional bodies, members' clubs can offer a huge return on investment if you work out what you need and find one that offers this. These are the elements I looked for in a members' club and enjoyed working out of London's *Hospital Club* once a week or more for several years:

- A helpful reception desk to meet and greet your clients and a cloakroom facility
- Rooms available to hire for meetings
- A lovely bar and restaurant for entertaining
- Events and networking opps to help your learning and business development
- A vibe and brand that feels aligned with yours

As the concept of a members' club has evolved over time, there is more choice and so it's worth taking the time to look around and find a club with vibes that resonate with your values and interests. Clubs tend to have restaurants and bars and the spaces to work are often sofas and cafe-style tables rather than desks, while co-working spaces tend to be more about desk-space and creating a funky office environment, but I do see the two types of memberships blending more, with shared workspaces becoming more sociable and members' clubs (such as Allbright) holding business pitch days with investors for example.

Co-working spaces and shared offices can offer a lot of the benefits of a private members' club, but are more focused on the day job and offering desk space and meeting rooms than a members' club, which tend to be more about the nightlife. If you can invest in both, then you have a great combination, but if you can only stretch to one, then think about what your biggest need is—do you want to grow a team? Then a co-working space is a wonderful, flexible way to do this. The smaller ones tend to be incredibly fun and have a lot of personality too. I worked out of *Huckletree* for some time, and their values about the environment and sustainability echoed my own, plus they were super flexible as our team expanded. *Huckletree* is more of a community than a co-working space, and the benefits are far-reaching, with members supporting each other in formal and informal ways as well as receiving inspiration and encouragement from the founders.

Gabriela Hersham of *Huckletree* explains:

Huckletree is a lively community of brave entrepreneurs. Our hubs are focused around different sectors such as GovTech; Venture Hubs; and Digital Lifestyle, for example. We run accelerator programmes to 'super-charge' entrepreneurs seeking funding. If you're thinking a co-working space is just a desk space, think again, because yes of course you can rent desks and sign up for mailbox services and so on, but the real benefit comes from the butterfly effect when members start to interact with one another—and we facilitate that and curate our community.

What you might want to consider when choosing a co-working space:

- The commute from your home: if it's too far, you simply won't go (you know it's true!)
- The ethos of the company
- The price: this can of course vary wildly, so do some research
- Whether the actual space suits your needs: if it's open plan, consider asking about NDAs (non-disclosure agreements) as you don't want another business sitting next to you listening to your ideas—this may sound a tad paranoid, but keeping your IP confidential is important to you and your clients, so think about who can hear your phone conversations
- The theme of the space: is it aimed at other people like you, and is there a good mixture of like-minded people without too many direct competitors?

Essentially all of these spaces and support networks can help you learn and grow and can also offer you the chance to be in a city center without the expense of a regular office rent. If your goal is to grow beyond being a one-person freelance operation to a boutique agency, for example, then shared spaces can be a brilliant option.

Money

Money means different things to everyone. You may not even realize your subconscious views about money which you could have picked up at a young age, either from your parents or family members or other influential people around you. Setting up on your own could be about financial freedom in terms of turning away from the corporate world, or it could be the chance to build up your own empire and make a million. Whatever your financial goals, facing and talking about money is inevitable when you set up a freelance business or consultancy.

- Think about how you will charge for your services or products or time: you may wish to benchmark this against others in your industry or in comparable industries
- Work backward from what you need in order to cover your bills or overheads or salary or taxes and have a generous contingency fund: then calculate how much you need to earn each week or month or year in order to fulfil these needs and goals
- Work out how you will charge and choose how you will talk about money with your clients: this could include whether you charge upfront or after the service or product has been provided, whether there is a cancellation policy, whether you will offer discounts and what you will do if someone doesn't pay

Once you've established your approach to money and pricing, work out which parts you are going to handle yourself and what you'd prefer to outsource. Some freelancers love nothing better than to watch a graph showing their income making a positive trajectory over the weeks and months, while others are happy letting someone else take the reins and check in with you when something needs attention.

I spoke again to Emma Maslin, aka *The Money Whisperer*, who explained that a lot of it—our relationship with money—comes down to confidence:

People say: 'I'm not good at maths' and that's how they excuse not being any good with money, but being good with money and maths aren't related at all. Not everyone has the same level of knowledge about basic financial literacy. My parents always talked to me about money when I was growing up, but we're not taught about personal finance or how to negotiate at school.

A lot of it's in our brain, it's our mindset. We've put blocks in our way and we say 'oh it's too hard', and we just go along doing the things that are in our comfort zone, and the things that we know, and that we're happy with. So coaching for me was a way of helping people explore their own personality, understand their beliefs around money and where those beliefs come from.

Emma and I talked about some of the blocks facing creative freelancers around themes such as pricing and invoicing—putting a value on time and allocating a worth to our creative work. She says:

Everything around how we view money, and also about putting ourselves out there, is all a function of what is going on in our brains. All the stories and the scripts that our little internal voice tells us in our ear is fairly well molded by the time we're about seven years old, which is what a lot of research shows. It's about uncovering and discovering what happened in our formative years that embedded those beliefs about self-worth and charging.

And for quite a lot of people it's not necessarily even about money. When it comes to money and spending for example, you get people who might binge eat or might restrict their eating—that's never about food, it's always about something else, it's about control. This is the same with money—it's a function of control. When you feel out of control you bury your head in the sand and the natural thing to do is to say 'I don't want to send the invoice' and/or 'I don't want to chase the invoice', and that's a reflection of feeling out of control and choosing the easy path, which is to ignore.

It's symbolic in other areas of life—food is another really great parallel.
You can choose what you can and can't control, and you focus on that
and you ignore the underlying problem that's causing you anxiety or
worry. When you look back at your formative years there is typically
a trigger; I trained as a TimeLine therapist to be able to support my
clients to uncover that trigger as often their conscious mind doesn't
know what the trigger is. So for all of these things, the way that we
behave is a function of habit usually. About 95% of things that we
do in a day are subconscious, we don't choose to do them, we just do
them. The positive change comes when you can unpick the bad habits
and relearn good ones.

The conversation with Emma really opens up the idea that our relationship with money can be incredibly emotional, and when we combine
that with charging for our creative work and our sense of value around
our work, it can be a deep and complicated process. Sending an invoice
can become a whole subconscious dialogue with ourselves about our own
worth. By working with a coach such as Emma, we might find that uncovering where the blocks are and re-framing our attitude about money and
finance could in fact free up a lot of time and energy and also help us see
an increase in the flow of money coming into our lives.

In the meantime, while we are doing this work around our money
mindset, there are some really easy practical steps we could take to make
sure we stay on track, despite any blocks we may have.

Annie Browne of *Hello My PA* says if money is a block for you, then
a great option could be to outsource it. For her, it was not about burying
her head in the sand; in fact she became really caught up in focusing too
much on the flow of money through her business. She explains:

I struggled a lot with money blocks at the start of my business, spend-
ing more time than I needed to focus on what was coming in and out,
sending invoices and watching for payments. My bookkeeper/accoun-
tant takes control of that for me now and their experience and focus
means that they spend a lot less time doing it than I ever did. I don't
have to think about it, giving me head space to be more creative and
more time to work in my business.

If outsourcing really isn't an option and bookkeeping and accounts software seem out of budget, many of the big name banks have software included to send invoices and track income. Be sure to use one of these when you set up your business bank account.

Outsourcing to a trusted professional is definitely one way of approaching freelance finances, if they are a struggle for you. Another is to face the challenge head-on, engaging a money coach to identify what it is about money that feels uncomfortable, and develop a fresh mindset— bringing more money and a sense of ease around this taboo topic. In fact it can be such a taboo topic that research by Capital Group in 2018 revealed that Americans "would rather talk about anything other than money, including marriage problems, mental illness, drug addiction, race, sex, politics and religion"[1].

Lacking a vocabulary or confidence around money can seriously put us on the back foot as clients can choose to exploit this and non-payment runs rife in the creative freelance world. Recent research by MarketInvoice (now known as MarketFinance) showed that 48 percent of the invoices in the creative sector are paid late[2]—that's almost half, and adds up to more than a billion pounds owed, which suggests we literally cannot afford to be shy about money.

Freelancers often find themselves chasing invoices via the exact same contacts who give them work and recommend them, which can lead to a fear of burning bridges and the flow of work from that client drying up. Having a clear agreement at the start can help to keep the conversation professional. Asking for part, or complete, payment up front can eliminate the problem and works well with consultancy work such as running training sessions.

Money expert Helen Fleet is a chartered accountant in Manchester, UK, who works as an outsourced Finance Director for a portfolio of clients—predominantly with growth businesses. Helen's worked in

---

[1] https://capitalgroup.com/about-us/news-room/americans-would-rather-talk-about-anything-besides-money-capital-group-survey-finds.html

[2] https://marketfinance.com/blog/marketfinance-news/2019/03/11/creative-industries-on-ice-waiting-for-gbp1b-in-late-payments

finance for more than 20 years, with senior roles in manufacturing and professional services. She shares some vital tips for getting paid on time and managing cash flow:

How to get paid on time

- Ensure you agree payment terms upfront.
- Find out who will be authorizing your invoices for payment—is it your contact or will it go to a finance team.
- Ensure you have a contact name for someone in the finance team, if applicable.
- If it's a large organization you are dealing with, find out if they have a payment run on a monthly basis and when that is—if it's the end of the month you may need to get your invoices in a week before the payment run date.
- If it's a small organization, be up front at the start and ask if they envisage any issues with prompt payment and whether they think your payment terms are achievable.
- After you've sent in your first invoice, phone and check after a couple of days that they have received it and it has been approved—this saves time when the due date arrives and also prevents customers using lack of approval as an excuse when the payment falls due.

How to approach payment terms:

- Consider what is the norm for your industry—payment on receipt, on 14 days or 30 days. If the normal is 30 days and you put 14 on your invoices, customers are likely to ignore it and your cash flow projections will be out of sync.
- If it's a lengthy project, can you agree to staged payments—this could be based on completion of certain stages within the project or based on a certain number of hours spent. At best, ask if you can secure a percentage up front.

Tips on chasing payment:

- Chase payment as soon as the invoice falls due.
- If they can't pay now, then ask for a payment date; if they won't give you one, say you will phone back in two days for a payment date.
- If they give you a payment date, make sure you follow up if they don't pay.
- If you have followed the right procedures on dealing with a new customer, then you should have the right contact name to chase.
- Always phone first and then follow up with confirmation of what you have discussed via e-mail. Chaser e-mails without an initial phone call are easily ignored.
- Set diary reminders or use your accounting software or related apps to remind you when to chase.

How to manage your cash flow:

- A client once told me that they felt like they didn't plan their cash flow enough but in other ways they felt like they thought of nothing else. Setting time aside each month to do this will get rid of this feeling and bring some order. If you hate doing it, then at least it is confined to one day per month.
- Keep a simple calculation of income and expenditure.
- Jot down what your outgoings are for the next three months.
- At the end of each month, update your expected income based on due dates.

She concludes: "If you do this regularly each month it will mean half an hour spent doing this saves you lots of time fretting during the month wondering where you are at."

Security and choice

IPSE (A UK-based membership body, which exists to support independent professionals and the self-employed), carried out a chunky piece of research in 2018, called *The Path to Prosperity*, exploring what can be done to make freelancing sustainable, fulfilling and financially rewarding. They found that:

> For the self-employed overall, 'financial wellbeing' means being in a state of financial security that gives them choice in their career and the freedom to enjoy life—as well as the ability to provide for family and loved ones and feel secure in their financial future.[3]

When choosing whether to go freelance, or how to work as an independent practitioner, financial wellbeing is one of the most significant factors. Weighing up the (relative) security of having an employer who provides holidays, health insurance, a pension and sick pay, versus having to take responsibility for all of that by yourself, is a huge consideration, especially if you have dependents.

Security and choice were the two biggest factors that freelancers and self-employed people named in the study, when it comes to financial wellbeing. Financial freedom is the path to both of those—being able to have choices, and that security—not just for ourselves—but for those we love and care for too.

So what are the barriers here, preventing self-employed people being able to enjoy the financial freedom they crave? Interestingly, one of the key obstacles highlighted in the study pointed to financial advice tailored to the self-employed. Sitting alongside this is the depressing reality of clients not paying on time, or, in some cases, not paying at all:

"Research by the IPA showed that 63 per cent of the self-employed have suffered from late payment, while 43 percent have, in some instances, not been paid for their work at all."[4]

---

[3] https://ipse.co.uk/resource/the-path-to-prosperity.html
[4] IPA, *Working Well for Yourself*, July 2018

Seek out professional financial advice

While the IPSE study claimed that a lack of tailored financial advice wasn't easy to find, I believe it is there if you seek it out. However, I agree that it's not as easy to find as consumer advice, so for example you may have to make an appointment instead of just strolling into a bank, if you want to speak to their small business specialist. Ways to gain support with your finances could involve one, or all, of the following:

- Get yourself a financial adviser. (I've had one since I was in my 20s.)
- Get over any squeamishness around talking about money. Where I live, in the UK, money has always been seen as one of the themes never to raise at a dinner party (alongside politics and religion), but by pushing it into that *no-go* area, it's left many of us without the vocabulary or understanding around how to manage money, how to talk about it and what to do if we don't have enough of it. Not having money has, for so long, been linked with *shame* in our minds that if we are not paid as freelancers, we may start thinking we are not good enough instead of thinking about how to solve the non-payment problem.
- Create a financial plan: whether that's a business plan or simply an annual budget for your freelance work, you will know how much you need to earn, which will help you to set your financial goals for your business and inform your new business strategy too.
- Hire an accountant. Accountants are not only great at keeping you within the law and making sure your finances are in order, they can also be super helpful when it comes to challenges such as getting a mortgage as a freelancer, or providing a reference for you if you are making a significant financial commitment. Doing your finances yourself is often a false economy as accountants can help you to save money, by being aware of the latest tax breaks and opportunities—meaning they essentially pay for themselves

Lessons learned in financial downturn

Dan Simon is a creative entrepreneur who knows a thing or two about finance: he's the CEO and co-founder of financial PR firm *Vested*, and author of the HarperCollins book *The Money Hackers*. He's also created a popular podcast, written for *Forbes* and earlier in his creative career was even in a boy band! Dan's someone I call when I'm stuck and want a completely different perspective or some *tough love*-style business or comms advice. He's straight-talking and unafraid of speaking about money, despite being a British guy working and living in New York (unusual because us Brits are stereotypically all euphemisms). Over the years, he's witnessed epic failures in the financial world.

Dan was hired to start the U.S. arm of his previous firm at the beginning of the 2008 financial crash. He explained the mindset that helped them grow when huge businesses were physically closing all around them. And the lessons he learned enabled him to start up *Vested*, his own financial communications firm—in New York and London—which he's co-created with two savvy business partners. They share his positive, energetic and pragmatic mindset. He said:

> *I remember standing outside the Lehman (now Barclays) building watching that huge wraparound LCD screen flicker and then go dark. I was 29 years old and I didn't know whether my career was taking off or had ended before it began.*

He saw this youth as an asset, and the fact that he was in the industry that was at the center of the storm as a benefit too in some ways, in the sense he knew what he was dealing with, even though it was scary.

> *Perversely I think if I'd been in a different industry or somewhere other than Wall St I would have been a lot more scared but we were right in the thick of it and the buildings were still standing, cabs driving, people drinking in bars so you kind of knew we'd get through it.*

> *Partly the message there is be fearless. Which is terrible advice because in essence you're saying "try to be 29 with no responsibilities or com-*

mitments whatsoever" but having less to lose and being more open to opportunities was definitely beneficial at the time. Warren Buffett is fond of saying: "Be fearful when others are greedy and greedy when others are fearful."

What happened next reminds me a little of the scene in the film Jerry Maguire when Tom Cruise's character is ringing around his clients trying to hold on to them, having left his job with only a goldfish to his name. Dan hammered the phones explaining to clients that they needed PR now more than ever and that staying on board would enable them to get through this and come out the other side. Writing this makes me go a little cold and yet feel energized too, as the financial crash was the exact time in my own life when I lost my job in financial PR (through redundancy) and started working for myself. Dan explained his mindset to me, and what he learned:

Regarding the clients there was no great trick, no Jedi mind control—we were small and scrappy which meant we could undercut the other guys on cost—even as they were scaling back their programs—and from a new business perspective we had never had anything come to us so were less psychologically impacted if that makes sense. I think that was super beneficial during the downturn. Many other agencies had relied on their reputation and size to drive inbound new business calls through good times. They literally had no idea what to do when the phones stopped ringing. Conversely, the phones had never started ringing for us, so we barely noticed a difference.

Someone once said "happiness equals expectation minus reality." If your expectation is tons of leads and the reality is only a single lead, your agency is in misery. If your expectation is no leads and you get one lead, your agency is having a party.

Knowing the people who signed off spending and made the actual decisions made all the difference to Dan at that difficult time, and helped him to win through. This is a lesson for anyone working creatively and running their own operation—know who is *actually* paying you and approving your plans, fees and costs. If your main contact is someone who has no decision-making power, then do some work to embed yourself higher up in the structure (and make yourself invaluable). Dan told me:

> *I think the other thing that helped us—and which we learned from - is that our clients were smaller financial technology providers. This meant we were much closer to the business heads—the CEO and their team—which meant we were able to demonstrate and defend the results of PR without having to go through a CMO (Chief Marketing Officer) or CCO (Chief Commercial Officer). This meant that when times were tough we were able to show how the work we did was critical to their future success. Many agencies who reported into marketing and comms functions inside the big financials were cut almost immediately because they didn't have that direct connection. It's correlated to that earlier point about new business. If your CMOs and CCOs have thick budgets which you're used to taking without questioning and you don't much care where the budget comes from (at the end of the day it's the business side) then when you face a downturn those big, new mandates are going to dry up and the CMOs are going to lose their jobs and you will get cut in turn. So it's a double whammy.*

> *We were already lean and scrappy so any leads we secured were great and we weren't big enough like those fancy agencies to be hired or considered by those big CMOs / CCOs which was just as well!*

> *As we've started and grown Vested we've been keen to keep close to the business side even inside firms with big comms teams. Morgan Stanley wealth management for example we love the comms team but took the CEO and COO of the business plus their spouses to dinner at this incredible restaurant on Saturday and have a date round the CEO's house in the coming weeks.*

Dan summarized his approach:

- Keep a lean mindset—even as you grow
- Stay very close to the business side, that is, figure out and latch on to whoever pays the person that pays you
- Take nothing for granted—practice healthy paranoia
- Always be closing—hustle and don't rely on inbound business solely

I asked Dan, what exactly did he say to his clients at this incredibly difficult time?

I said you need it [PR] now more than ever. But again it was partly who I was talking to. Because we were engaging directly with the business side we were better able to make our case. We also focused much more on business outcomes in those conversations. PR/marcomms couldn't just be about top of funnel brand stuff. We had to show a commitment to delivering business outcomes.

CHAPTER 8

Love your clients

Being freelance or a new start-up is not an excuse for not having a customer service policy—yeah, sorry I know, you thought you'd got away with it! Having a clear approach and strategy to customer service may be even more important to a small business or freelance operation because word-of-mouth is such a strong source of clients, plus your customers are more likely to be buying into *you*, the owner, and *you* the person rather than a brand. No pressure! At the same time, you are likely to find that goodwill is more abundant among customers of small businesses because there is that personalization. Getting the balance right between being authentic and professional can be tricky. If your cleaner's son has chickenpox and he or she has to stay home, then you would understand but you still need your house cleaned, the job still has to get done. It's no different for creative freelancers—the deadline still applies, so having a process will stand you in good stead. Perhaps you have a network of trusted freelancers who can support you if you're unwell, or a reciprocal arrangement with another agency for getting work done if you're not available. Future-proofing your business might also help you feel secure about your ability to provide great customer service even if you're unwell or maxed out.

When thinking about client servicing as a creative freelancer, you may wish to consider the following elements:

- *Clarifying the brief:* Before you begin a new project, let's all be clear on the deliverables and timescales, it's very easy to become absorbed in and distracted by the creativity itself and know when to stop and deliver the work on time! You may wish to have a template form for the client to fill in or hold a face-to-face or phone meeting where you interrogate the brief. Once the brief is agreed, then work out what the actual deliverables are. If, for example, you are creating brand guidelines and a color palette, aim to physically sign off the finished product by an agreed deadline, especially if you're going back and forth with various versions. Don't leave it up in the air.

- One of my favorite clients who I offer consultancy services to will not only agree milestones in the project, they will also agree a phased payment system whereby I get paid when I hit each milestone. I find this incredibly motivating, and there's something very tangible about the payment hitting my bank account that makes it clear to everyone that we're happy with where we are.

- *Deadlines and feedback:* Some copywriters specify how many rounds of changes they will take on board within their costing. If the project starts to take longer and involve more than, say, two rounds of changes, then higher costs could be incurred. Making this type of thing clear as part of your contractcan protect your time and help you meet the deadlines. This is also likely to help the client by encouraging them to specify their changes in one go! Make it as easy as possible for your client to give honest feedback, without emotions getting in the way. Some of the feedback will help you to grow and develop, and some of it will not be personal but be about getting the best fit for the brief. As a client, asking if the creative freelancer can think of any ways they'd like to improve the work can really open things up. Sometimes I've found the brief I have provided has been too restrictive and prevented them being able to produce their best work. I've also discovered that if my deadlines are genuinely not fixed, that allowing a creative extra time can really help develop the project. So whether you are on the side of the client or you are the creative, giving the project space to breathe can be beneficial.

- *How do they like to work?* There are plenty of articles about the importance of having boundaries as a freelancer, and maintaining a flexible workstyle, but understanding how the client likes to work is vital too of course. Setting your own stall out around your working practices is completely professional, but I'd say be prepared to make some compromises too. If you are too rigid about only using one particular type of software or the format of your meetings, for example, you may discover that locks you out of a lot of valuable and nourishing opportunities. Finding out how the client prefers to work and checking-in with them every so often, is just a good business practice.

o Clients are likely to reflect back to you the way you approach them. And at the same time, you may find each other's worlds are a bit of a mystery! You've connected precisely because they do not have the skills or expertise to do what you do, so we can't make assumptions that our acronyms or jargon makes any sense to someone outside our world. Make it easy for them to be a good client: by all means offer them a different way of working, but also offer them the chance to blend that with the way they like to receive information and give feedback.

- *Who is the client?* This may sound like a weird question, but anyone who has worked on a creative project is likely to know that, no matter who commissions the work, when you get to the sign-off or payment stage other names often seem to crop up! Your client's colleague or brother or business advisor may suddenly get called in, or the board may be consulted. Finding out at the start who has the final sign-off and who is paying the bill can save tears later and also help with client management. Reminding the responsible individual that it's actually on them to make the decision can help create focus. And how sign-off is gained can be worth some thought too. Is it a physical signature or something else? How will you capture it? A text saying *ok* on an expensive project may not create enough of an audit trail, should things go wrong.

Ways to avoid client unhappiness

- *Share work-in-progress* so the client can see and feed back on the direction of your thinking before it's too late! This also enables them to collaborate with you, in a non-hierarchical way.
- *Establish the brief* and your response to it at the start—defining what success looks like to everyone involved.
- *Agree sign-off procedures*—and have an awareness of who the buck stops with. If there is a *board-level* approval process at the end, then it really helps to know who those people are and—if possible—meet them beforehand to build rapport and understand their thinking and priorities.
- *Explain how you work* upfront. And agree how you will all communicate too. With so many different forms of digital communication available, establish your or their boundaries around communicating. Understanding this can eliminate being an annoyance and equally avoid being seen as elusive.

Terms of business or contracts

To get things rolling, the easiest way to define your terms of business or contract at the start is almost always to use a template. Unless you have the budget to fork out on a lawyer or happen to be a legal expert, a template can be a quick and easy way to get started. It's also worth checking what type of insurance you might need and reading the small print there so that you comply with that too. Once you are up and running, revisit your terms of business every few months. How will you know what to add? Well, that might come from the list of things that have gone wrong!

Paul Clarke is a friend of mine and also an incredibly skilled photographer. He's one of the people I consider to be in my squad of other creative independent business owners. He describes his terms of business as a "graveyard of things that have gone wrong." I love everything about this. The honesty, the learning and how smart he is. While a lot of us will be tempted to move quickly past those things that didn't go well, he gets them out on the table, looks at them and thinks "how could this be useful to me?" and notices those things that went wrong, which were out of his control, and where there is probably something he can do and put in place in order not to make the same mistake again. He explains:

I'll give you an example - one thing I used to get really stung by: a PR company would call up and book a job and give me the brief, and I'd go off and I'd do the job and I'd send them the pictures, and then I'd try and get them to pay. They would say 'oh well we aren't paying you, it's our client that's paying you'. It's easy to spot and evaluate the problem there.

So paragraph number 1 of my terms of business is now headed 'confirmation of client'. Which means at the time when you give out any brief you make it absolutely clear who's commissioning—not just to say how you're getting paid but who's giving you direction as well—because what happens when the brand marketer comes to the shoot and starts telling you this, and the PR's saying this, and the journalist is going 'I don't wanna do any of this', you're in the middle.

So that's a simple example where a series of bad experiences led to a simple form of words which was: you have to tell me who I'm being directed by and who's paying and ideally [that will be] the same people.

Customer service

Annie Browne, virtual assistant and owner of *Hello My PA* is passionate about customer service. And she's also a huge advocate of remote working. She told me:

The value of customer experience in business growth is something I could write about at length. In a nutshell though, the way that an individual experiences your brand, your business and the service you provide, is completely independent of your physical proximity to them.

The key to all round great customer service and client experience is effective communication on every level; the way you express your company values via social media, advertising and your customer-facing representatives, the way that you talk and listen to your customers to discover what they want and how they feel, the way that you use that information to deliver their ideal product or service and the way that you make your clients or customers feel valued and comfortable.

I also place huge value in nurturing relationships with clients by setting expectations right from the start and consistently meeting those expectations. For some clients, they like to meet face-to-face occasionally, for others a monthly catch up on the phone is what works and for one particular client, in the four years we have worked together, we have never had a conversation on the phone. We have only ever emailed.

A problem only really occurs with your customer service when an expectation of your brand, company, product or service is not met and is consequently not rectified; the latter being the key point. If you don't meet an expectation and you rectify it, you are upholding a service dedicated to the customer. If you constantly don't meet expectations, something is wrong with either the expectations you are setting or your processes in meeting them.

To summarise; develop great communication skills, set expectations from the start of every relationship and meet them and when a problem arises, do what you can to fix it and assess what went wrong so that it is unlikely to happen again.

And having great client relationships relies on—sometimes—being able to broach tricky subjects and say the unsayable. As a consultant or expert, you are not simply a do-er. If you are a do-er, then you are unlikely to be reaching your creative potential for yourself or giving your client the best value. This doesn't mean changing and contradicting everything the client asks of you, but having the confidence to make insightful suggestions in order to get the best results for everyone.

Learn to have difficult conversations

If you want to thrive as a consultant, then learning to have difficult conversations sooner rather than later will serve you well. This essential skill will help you to attract more money to your business, allow you to feel more comfortable and confident in your skin and develop ease and honesty in your interactions.

Cath Brown who runs the business *Skilful Conversation* bases her coaching, training and workshops on managing difficult conversations on her 15 years' experience as a personal injury barrister, having difficult conversations with judges, clients, solicitors and clerks. She's been coaching for five years. Cath explains:

> *I absolutely agree with you that thinking about how and where to have the [difficult] conversation is vital, that in person is preferable, and that email can be vital for setting up that conversation and expectations around it, and for ensuring that the outcome is recorded. Although I would add that actually face-to-face can be too much for some people with some subjects, and they can really benefit from having that chat in person but not face-to-face.*

Cath suggests that walking and talking may be a way to achieve an in-person conversation, without being directly opposite the other person. In Cath's experience, attempting to do the important or the difficult by e-mail can lead to clumsiness and misunderstandings. She says:

> *The recipient of the email will apply their own interpretation rather than asking for more details or a better understanding as they probably would face-to-face.*

> *Being there while the conversation takes place allows you to adapt, think on your feet and make real progress, rather than to-ing and fro-ing over email, message after message. It allows you to use non-verbal indicators – tone of voice, changes in breathing, pauses and so on – so that you can gauge much more accurately whether the meaning of*

what you're saying is hitting the mark, and what the other person is thinking. It allows for much more real human connection and rapport and makes it much less likely that the conversation will end badly.

Cath's advice for having difficult conversations effectively:

- Having the difficult conversation is not nearly as bad as you think it will be.
- The more you do it, the easier it gets—so take the opportunity to practice having difficult conversations!
- Think about the benefit it will bring you, once you've had the conversation: for example, if you've not been paid, or you don't understand the brief. Doing nothing may feel like the safe option, but doing nothing will not benefit you if it means you're then unable to pay your bills.
- We sometimes assume the other person knows more than us or is an ogre, but often with nothing to base that on.
- Most of us are capable of having the conversation and will still be alive at the end of it!
- E-mail can be used as a shield that can remove social sensibilities! In person, people tend to be less mean or abrupt once that virtual shield is removed.
- E-mails are easy to ignore, so if you need the other person to take action, a conversation can be more effective.

"Don't let yourself off the hook—commit to having the conversation," she advises. And we also talked about the importance of reflection and feedback—have a think about what happened, did it go well and what might you do differently next time?

If you've come from a role in a larger business where you have someone to handle things like contracts, invoicing and finance for you, and now you're doing this all yourself, then it can be a big step to start taking on conversations about these sort of themes with clients. Cath acknowledges that in her previous role as a barrister, she didn't even have to talk about money as someone would do that for her. So as a new freelancer or founder it can sometimes be an obstacle to overcome. We suggest setting up the working relationship with your client to allow plenty of opportunity for conversation so that it does not feel like a big leap when you do have to bring up a tricky topic.

Conversely, Cath and I discussed the need to establish—for yourself—your desired outcome of the difficult conversation. You may just want to be heard, for example, but it is not really your client's job to make you feel better! If you just want to get something off your chest, then maybe speak to a friend, coach or therapist about it. However, if there is a genuine practical and business-led outcome that you need to get from the conversation, focus on that—whether it's getting paid or establishing a contract or defining a brief, for example. Cath explained that in many cases, someone might want to have a difficult conversation 'because of the principle of the thing' when in reality a check on what the commercial need is or was would help more. This is not to say that you should stand by if a client is going against your values and beliefs, but that you shouldn't offload just for the sake of it without a goal in mind. If you're just looking for an apology, maybe let this go.

Cath outlined some steps to take to help you focus on what you need to get from the difficult conversation:

- Think about what has happened
- What need that relates to for you?
- What your request is: tell them what you want and tell them why they should give it to you
- Make that request with clarity

And as a trained barrister herself, Cath also reminded me that what is written in an e-mail could one day end up in a courtroom and so this is also worth bearing in mind if you are entering into a dispute with a client, supplier or other business or individual. Be mindful of what you commit to writing.

From a coaching perspective, I think it's incredibly important to set up the environment for an honest conversation. In a coaching session, we always open with a brief contracting conversation and a check-in. By reminding ourselves of the confidentiality of our coaching conversation, and beginning with checking how the client is feeling today, we put ourselves in a strong position to talk about difficult topics. We also have a coaching contract, which sets out how we will interact with one another. Conversely, broaching a sensitive or difficult topic without creating the right conditions for it can be unhelpful, so I'd urge you when you do want to *say the unsayable* to think about what might be happening for the other person and what sort of agreement you have before blurting things out! Building a rapport and trust is vital to being able to be honest and constructive.

Flexible working and balance

The opportunity to work flexibly is one of the top reasons my clients give me for choosing to or wanting to go freelance. And what it means to be flexible has many different facets. Flexibility could mean:

- The hours or days you work
- Where you work from
- Setting your own prices
- Being able to say no to a project or task
- Who you work with
- Having the school holidays off
- Taking a sabbatical
- Working around an illness
- Having more than one focus

Annie Ridout is a successful journalist and author, writing about life-style and parenting. Her books include *The Freelance Mum* and she has a strong online profile that she uses thoughtfully to support and encourage her followers, with an openness and natural generosity.

I asked Annie if mums are choosing to freelance so that they can work more flexibly?

Yes, I've seen lots of women go freelance after having a baby. Perhaps they don't want to return to commuting, or haven't been granted the flexible working they're after, so they decide to set something up that they can do from home. This is what I hear from women who've read my book (The Freelance Mum) or done my courses.

Work-life balance is really important for everyone, but particularly once children come along, as lots of us want to be around more during their early years. It's not easy, freelancing as a mum— or without kids. There is the pressure to keep your workload up, it's tricky taking holidays without feeling you should be working and work and life do often blend. But for me, it's far better than going into an office full-time so I keep that in mind when I'm on the brink of complaining.

When employers do not offer flexibility, Annie says the only option for parents can be "wrap-around childcare," which can have its own drawbacks, even for parents who find it affordable.

"Ideally, everyone would be allowed to work flexibly; whether employed or self-employed. But we're far from that right now." She says.

When it comes to achieving good work/life balance, Annie advises putting strong boundaries in place:

I think it's hard for people to understand that just because you work from home, it doesn't mean you're always available for coffees and drop-ins. So creating clear boundaries is important. But also, taking proper breaks and holidays is crucial. I break every day for a proper lunch - lots of vegetables, hot food - and at Christmas, had a proper two-week break. We went to the countryside and walked in the fresh air and had such a lovely time. It reminded me of the importance of not constantly checking my phone and writing Instagram posts when on holiday.

Part of flexible working and work/life balance can be about tuning in to your uniqueness, and what you need to thrive. Annie is currently writing a book about shyness. She explains why:

I'm writing a book on shyness, and how it can be an attribute. I think we often frame shyness as a fault so I'm working to change this narrative—in the same way that 'introversion' is now socially accepted. Once upon a time, introversion was frowned upon, as shyness still is. I wouldn't say shyness is part of my brand, though. It's something that's there, and that I mention in case it helps others to feel less alone with similar feelings. Pretending that we're always confident and loud and love public speaking and never make mistakes is not my vibe—I'm all about openness and sharing the 'flaws' too.

Being able to take holidays and spend time with family—or being able to work independently, and tune in to our needs more—can often be a catalyst for those who go freelance. Once we are set up on our own though, it can be so easy to lose sight of our original goals as client demands take over. Ways to stay on track with our goals and boundaries include:

- Stating your goals out loud, keeping them displayed prominently or sharing them with a coach or mentor
- Reviewing each day and week in a journal and reflecting on decisions made and how closely they fit with your values and goals
- Making your holidays and working hours part of your client contracts and part of who you are as a company
- Setting up an *out of office* reply to let clients know well in advance when you are available, and sticking to it
- Charging extra for out-of-hours working… this will often discourage clients asking for weekend or evening working, and if it does happen, then you could use the extra cash to pay for things that make your life easier—such as taxis, a cleaner, a virtual assistant and so on

You will be able to think of plenty more ways that work for you, to help you stick to your boundaries, reach your goals and stay true to your values. The important thing to remember is, whatever does work for you, keep doing it consistently. If you are stop or start about implementing your boundaries, then clients will learn bad habits and feel like they can interrupt you any time.

CHAPTER 9

Work is not a place

"44% of remote workers travel while working between one week and one month per year, and 25% of respondents do this work/travel combination more than one month of the year"[1].

If you grew up in the 1980s like me, you might associate the word *work* with a place, a physical place you go. Mum, Dad and other adults and role models in your life perhaps went *to work* and they came home, took off their tie or work shoes and slid into family life. Work was an office, a site, or a mapped out area of the county. But was work really ever a place or was or is it something we do?

When I started *work* then, sharing articles meant photocopying them, and the office I began my comms career in had an internal train for the mail, which ran around 25 floors of the (then) tallest tower in Manchester, England. We had e-mail, but it was slow and clunky and speaking on the phone was our main way of communicating. We literally hammered those phones all day long and once a month went across to London to meet journalists and network. Work was a place, it was Manchester, it was a high-rise tower, there was breakfast and lunch provided (for free) to staff, way before trendy tech companies thought of this idea. We also had access to a florist and a bank and so on. Ideas that may seem *current* now were already a way of life. I was in the five-a-side football team and participated in charity events and open days, which gave the location an even greater sense of place for me. I had a mobile phone, but it was mainly for PR emergencies and for taking to London. We took it in turns to be *on duty*. Hours were calculated by a machine that we clocked in and out by, inserting a plastic key to register our presence. At the end of the month, if we'd worked enough hours, we could leave early. We usually took advantage of this on payday, when most of the office would head to the pub in small groups, at about 3 p.m.

---

[1] *Source*: The State of Remote Work 2019, by Buffer.

Why does this matter? Well *work* was a place for me in some ways. My presence in that space was literally calculated, and I was rewarded for spending sufficient hours in it. For many of us who started our careers this way, we have spent more time with work seeming to be a place and using the phrase "I'm at work" or "I'm not at work," than with the more recent idea of work being something that we can do from anywhere as creative freelancers, homeworkers and digital nomads.

If work still feels to you like it is a place, but you'd like to change your thinking, then ponder the following questions and ideas:

- What do you need to have or wear or think or do to feel that you are *at work*?
- Do you actually *want* to work remotely?
- Where might you work from (sometimes or often) that is not your home or office or workshop? Where would feel good and why?
- Can you work in an environment that says something about you or your brand? What might that look like? (So for example, a client of mine works with flowers, and we sometimes meet at the garden center).
- Alternatively, perhaps you always operate from different locations and you'd like to feel more grounded and designate a space as your workspace. What could that look like? What would it bring you, and what do you need to make this happen?
- How can you work remotely and keep your data, ideas and belongings safe and secure? What might you need to implement?

"Where am I?
Here.
What time is it?
Now."
Ram Dass

This powerful quotation appears on the front page of River Flow Yoga's website. River Flow is run by Graham Nolan, in Mid Wales, and we went for a walk together, to discuss the idea of work as a place. Graham believes that work is not a place and yoga is not something that only happens on a yoga mat. Yoga can be a way of life and can happen wherever you are. And creative work can involve having amazing ideas in the bath, for example. However, Graham explains:

> *It is vital to form strong boundaries if you subscribe to the idea that work can happen anywhere. Try to maintain your own practice once you have established this. If you enjoy it, then by all means work in bed, but if there are any parts of the job that you strongly dislike or even fear, don't bring those tasks into your relaxing spaces.*

Graham works independently and creatively himself, as a yoga teacher, sensory impairment specialist and also co-runs inspiring art events and retreats with his partner Matthew at their converted chapel home. He also believes that being a great yogi is not about how bendy you are but about mindset, and I think there is a lot that we can learn from this way of thinking. Being an effective founder or creative freelancer does not always have to hurt, and work does not always have to be in an environment that resembles the Dolly Parton movie 9 to 5, in fact she definitely had a point when she sang: "There's a better life, and you dream about it, don't you?"[2]

Being able to work from anywhere is one of the many reasons I'm such an advocate of freelancing and running your own business and I view it as a privilege. At the same time, the studio I often hire to meet my local clients is a wonderfully grounding place, beautiful and surrounded by woodland and next to a scenic river; it helps me create an ideal atmosphere for holding space while clients think.

Working overseas

Do you identify as a digital nomad? Are you an ex-pat? Maybe you work globally or simply live for your next holiday adventure. The freedom to travel can be a key motivator for many creative freelancers and a delicious advantage for those of us lucky enough to build our own schedule.

---

[2] Writer: Dolly Parton
Publisher: Sony/ATV Music Publishing LLC, DistroKid

If travel or relocation is a goal for you, but you're feeling tied to a client's office, with all the presenteeism that can sometimes enforce, it could be time to re-evaluate.

Julia Gutgsell is an ex-pat coach and mobility consultant, and she helps her globally minded clients navigate working and/or living overseas.

I asked her what inspired her to begin traveling and living in other countries. She explains:

> *When I was 14, I met a girl in my home town who was just a few years older than me, and she had just returned from Australia after being a foreign exchange student for a semester. I was really inspired by her story and decided that once I was her age I would want to become a foreign exchange student too. When I was 16, I started seriously researching it and initially it seemed almost an impossible feat, because exchange programs tend to be quite expensive and I didn't think my family would be able to afford it. So I combined two of my top strengths: perseverance and creativity, to design my own exchange program by finding a host family myself and a school that would host me. It turned out a lot cheaper than going through an organization - also a lot more work! In hindsight it was also quite a risky endeavor, considering I only knew my host family from our online interactions—luckily it all went well and paid off!*
>
> *Perhaps surprisingly, I'm not a huge fan of traveling. I love to stay in a place for a while and be immersed in it, I like exploring places off the beaten path, talk to locals and really understand the place. You can't do that in a couple of weeks or months. I still travel but I prefer being an expat and a bit more grounded and rooted in a place.*

I asked Julia what would be the one piece of advice she'd give to creative freelancers thinking about traveling as they work, or moving overseas?

> *Just do it! Don't get me wrong, I think preparation is really important but in my experience moving abroad can be a perpetual dream for*

many people and they get so lost in the preparation stage, wanting everything to be perfect that they get overwhelmed and end up being stuck in their home country. If you want to succeed and thrive in living a high mobility lifestyle you need to be willing to experiment and discover what works for you and what doesn't. Fail quickly and fail forward. And don't get discouraged by setbacks. Embrace them as opportunities for learning and self-discovery.

The idea of *failing forward* is about learning from mistakes, and this is also covered in more detail within Chapter 10.

One mistake that nobody will want to make will be around ensuring the right paperwork and plans are in place for your trip, whether that is visas, financial requirements, insurance or healthcare. Clearly it is different in each case and for each country, and following Julia Gutgsell's advice on this will stand you in good stead. She explains:

So, the first thing I suggest is to break down the move into stages: decision-making, preparation, arrival and integration. Breaking it down helps to make it more manageable and less overwhelming.

The decision-making stage is all about figuring out what your needs, preferences and goals are for moving abroad and short-listing countries that match those criteria. If you are moving with your family or a partner, also check how they feel. That is often overlooked and can create a lot of tension in relationships and even lead to separation. I also recommend visiting the place beforehand, whenever possible.

Preparation phase: research, research, research! Speak to freelancers who live in the country you want to go to and get first hand advice on what it's really like. If you can afford it, get professional business and relocation advice—a relocation company can help save you a lot of time, stress and money by managing the logistics and bureaucracy (such as: visa, work permits) for you, especially if you don't speak the language in the destination country. In terms of business advice the specifics will depend on the type of business you run, but at a minimum get an accountant, check if you need to register your business in the destination country and if so how, confirm your insurance is valid in the destination country.

Start growing your network abroad before you move. LinkedIn and similar platforms are great for connecting with professional contacts and getting a head start. Find out if the destination country offers specific services for freelancers and self-employed people that can provide information and signposting. Depending on where you are moving and how long you intend to stay I recommend starting at least six months earlier.

It can be tempting to just focus on your destination country and neglect to end things well locally: Create a list of all the services you use locally, your bills, post, check any contracts you have and how you can cancel them. Build an emergency fund. Arrange your accommodation. You might also need to revisit the fees you are charging for your work, this will largely depend on the costs of living in the host country or to adjust your prices if the local economy can't afford your prices, if you intend to work locally.

Arrival: don't jump straight into work. Give yourself some breathing space and settle in. Familiarize yourself with your surroundings and neighborhood. You might need time to adjust to a different time zone, language, and your senses might be overwhelmed by new noises, smells and tastes. Be kind to yourself. Once you are ready, start reaching out to the contacts you've made online, register with local services, start turning your accommodation into a home.

Some of my clients have found it useful to join co-working spaces to meet new people and make business contacts and to feel less isolated in a new place.

Integration: this is when your new place slowly starts to feel like home, your surroundings become more familiar, you have a network of people and you understand and can follow local customs. This can take a few months but, from my experience of working with expats, it's also not unusual for it to take up to a year or longer. As a rule of thumb, the more differences between your home culture and the host culture the longer it will take. Also the amount of previous international expe-

rience someone has will make a difference. The key to integration is consistency, find a routine that works for you, build habits and stick to them as much as possible.

I asked Julia what might be difficult about traveling as a freelancer on your own. She noticed that the difficulties for a freelancer traveling may in fact be very similar to what any freelancer might experience, regardless of the country they're working in:

In addition to the challenges faced by freelancers who are not traveling, one of the major challenges for traveling on your own is that you will have to sort out admin and bureaucracy on your own and learn to navigate a new place and culture on your own. This can lead to feeling isolated, lonely, feeling overwhelmed or confused. For some there are also financial worries if they have lost clients due to the relocation or if living costs in the host country are higher than the home country. The digital nomad lifestyle is often marked by high mobility, so the cycle of decision-making, preparation, arrival and integration are often followed in quick succession. This perpetual level of change and rootlessness can become very draining over time.

Building good mental health practises is absolutely crucial for dealing with those challenges. It's not necessary to reinvent the wheel, most of the strategies that worked back home, will work just as well abroad. Luckily, there are also many online resources and expat groups to reach out to for peer support and working with a coach can also help expats and digital nomads create that extra level of support and accountability. Digital nomads tend to spend large chunks of their day online, so finding opportunities to engage with people offline can introduce some balance.

And having covered some of the main challenges, I explored with Julia what is most rewarding about traveling. For me personally, I've found that whenever I'm in a new place, and a different culture, I literally have a sense of space and possibility, which stays with me after I return. In addition, I find inspiration and new ideas in unexpected places, as well as different attitudes, which help me think and create fresh perspectives.

For Julia, here are some of the key rewards for those freelancers who take their work overseas, she says:

There are personal and professional rewards. For me the biggest personal rewards have been self-discovery and the recognition that we humans are so much more alike than different. Traveling really puts you to the test. You discover strengths you never knew you had. It makes you adaptable, open, grateful and patient. You learn that there is no one-way or right way to live, because in your travels you discover that there's literally 1,000s of different 'right' ways of how to live your life. As a result, life choices tend to become more authentic and grounded in personal values.

From a professional perspective, it helps you stand out amongst other freelancers and generally that's a good thing. It can be a great ice-breaker when you meet a new client. Creative work is hugely impacted by personal experiences, so international experience is likely to add a unique perspective to how creatives approach their work.

Julia also cited this inspiring quote by Ibn Battuta:
"Traveling – it leaves you speechless, then turns you into a storyteller"
That's definitely another big reward! She says.

While living abroad and traveling as a freelancer can sound challenging, I want to emphasize that, in my experience of working with expats and my own personal experience, the positives far outweigh the challenges.

Digital nomads

Craig and Aimee literally gave up their day jobs to become digital nomads back in 2014. They do have a base, in their hometown of Barry, South Wales, and at the same time, they are able to travel across the world regularly, following both the trodden routes such as the east coast of Australia and less familiar routes such as Mongolia and Iran!

When Aimee was only 17, she contracted a form of cancer. At this young age, she had to undergo chemotherapy and was hospitalized for a time. Craig had his own life-changing moment when he broke his neck on a trip to New Zealand in his early 20s and so we have a couple where both individuals have experienced extreme life or death moments and rather than covering themselves in bubble wrap for the rest of their lives, they instead decided to dedicate their lives to adventure!

Craig and Aimee's experiences made the pair realize they did not want to become stuck in corporate life, they wanted to take control and explore, be in charge of their own destinies as much as possible and so they came up with the idea of *Kinging-It*. A brand, an ethos and a lifestyle. Firstly they *did* go into corporate jobs to save for a year and then they had a plan to implement, which they had researched and which many of their friends had told them would never work! They planned to become vloggers and YouTube stars . . . which was a relatively new phenomenon at that time, and combined Craig's photography skills and both of their creativity with new skills that they had to learn on the job.

I spoke to them both about their journey and what goes into being digital nomads. I suspect this is a dream for many, so I really wanted to get under the skin of what it's like in practice, behind the sun-filled photos many of us associate with this dreamy lifestyle!

As freelancers and business owners, there can often be a struggle with boundaries around when work *ends* and life *starts*, and working from home can make that tricky, but if you are on the road as a couple like Craig and Aimee are for the majority of their work, having boundaries is just so vital. They explain:

> *To travel, and work, as a couple we need patience. Massively. And time as well. It's having clear boundaries. If tomorrow is a day off then we just spend the time together without filming and just enjoy each other's company.*
>
> *Which up until very recently we've got wrong. We've got completely wrong.*

And the honesty and openness with which Craig and Aimee approached this was fantastic because they created a video blog for their followers about how they had couples counseling. This was not a paid promotion (and I say this because I have seen couples video blogging about counseling for a promotion, but this was not the case here). They noticed that to travel, they really needed to take care of their mental health and their relationship and so when they reflected back on how much counseling had helped them, they made this part of their story. The authenticity they approached it with, I think will really help and inspire other, less experienced bloggers and vloggers. And I think it makes their journey feel more inspiring. Personally, as a follower of their account and their story, I am just as interested to know this stuff as I am to see a beautiful monument or breathtaking landscape. Aimee explains the importance of good communication:

> We've been doing this since 2014 now and we have our own minds and own ideas and sometimes we do clash. So, we need to say 'this is my thought process, and this is why I think this will work' and try and speak verbally and try to figure out what's best to do.

The couple really noticed when you work for yourself, it's hard sometimes to have those boundaries between what's your work and what's your life, especially if you're putting a lot of that out there. And they've started to build some boundaries around free time versus creating content:

> It has to be done doesn't it because we've got a habit of just working all the time even if it's like just a couple of hours a day it will be every day. So yes we really need to put into place – the work needs to stop and we need to have time to enjoy ourselves and enjoy each other and give our heads a break.

> To the point where if one of us is like 'did you send that email', I'm like 'Are you talking about work?!!!'

So they've established permission with each other to call a time-out on work. And even if you are traveling alone and not as part of a couple or work partnership, then the idea of calling a time-out can be so vital.

I have traveled plenty while writing this book and coaching my clients. In terms of the practicalities of working as a digital nomad, here are some vital things to consider, which may sound obvious, but it's easy to forget in the excitement of the adventure itself.

- Planning
  While the idea of just taking each day as it comes sounds appealing, then planning and looking ahead will just reduce stress so much and also help you to avoid regret. For example, perhaps there are people in your network living in, or near, where you plan to visit, and connecting with them might make the trip even more fun. So you may want to reach out to people in advance of booking your journey. Creating an itinerary for yourself, even if it's just for you, is something I'd strongly suggest.

- Journaling
  Journaling has several purposes when you're traveling. It can help mental health and focus, keep you on track with client work and logistics and also help you to remember what you did and where you went if jetlag sets in and everything becomes a bit blurry!

- Pack thoughtfully
  While the essentials you take on holiday are fairly obvious, if you're working as you travel, they become more important. I spent a long time tracking down a UK to U.S. adapter when I omitted to pack mine, because the electrical shops all sold the opposite adapters, not the one I needed. Being unafraid to ask is sensible too though, in the end, my Airbnb host simply gave me one!

- Time difference
  Working with your existing clients across a time difference, without forward-planning can mean getting up at 4 a.m. or trying to have a meeting at 10 p.m. if you're not careful. If you often work across time zones, you'll be well used to it, but think ahead to what this means in practice and adapt accordingly. I actually like getting all my UK meetings out of the way in the early morning when I am in the United States and having the rest of the day free to explore.

- Pitstops

  While traveling alone can be really life-giving, arranging a few social coffees with people you met online or in person can help provide punctuation to your travels. I have a friend who works at Google for example, and so having breakfast with her in the middle of a week of solo traveling was a lovely pitstop and also gave me a bit of purpose around my trip too.

- Sightseeing

  For me, seeing the obvious sights is not my priority. For some people, they will want to tick the famous ones off the list, but I prefer finding unusual and less commercialized attractions. So for example, when I went to Brooklyn, I visited The Sketchbook Project, rather than only going to larger galleries. Not only are smaller attractions often free, for me there is also more of a story too.

- Modes of transport

  The cheapest or most obvious way to get from A to B might not always be the most fun! Ask around about the different ways to travel certain routes and you might find some exciting options that you've not thought of before. If the purpose of your journey is to enjoy traveling, a slower and more scenic route could bring more joy and inspiration.

- Networking

  What do you want to get out of your trip when it comes to widening your network? Is it about reconnecting with yourself and/or others? Do you want to meet new people, and how can you put yourself in a place to do that? What do you need to make that happen? Is it about building your trip around a conference or event and planning it out from there, or a retreat or to get a project started or completed? I've taken this book with me to several different countries, but in truth, I didn't write so much there as I did when I got back, it helped unblock some blocks, but the time I spent was about thinking and making space rather than putting words on the page.

- Focal points

  It can be fun to have a focus for your trip, I'm thinking of themes that drive me such as food and art, or music. As well as having an itinerary, I tend to build each day's schedule in my journal when I'm traveling, and brunch features highly! While I do still have phone and video meetings while traveling, I suggest reducing the amount of slots you make available to clients because sitting in an Airbnb missing the whole day can be a bit of a disappointment!

- Keeping clients on side

  However fun and empowering it is to travel, let's not take a working vacation at the expense of our clients. Communicate well with your clients in advance, to let them know you'll be in a different time zone. Put an out-of-office on your e-mail if you anticipate a slow reply (especially on days when you are flying), and rejig your schedule around to make it work for your clients and yourself. This will make your traveling experience more enjoyable and keep your clients feeling reassured and calm.

- Making it work for you

  For me, keeping up some of my own routines can be useful even when traveling; it can help me to feel grounded and maintain good mental health. If you have therapy every week, then consider building that time into your schedule too, or visiting a retreat on your travels to take part in some yoga or meditation—whatever works for you.

CHAPTER 10

Fail forward

Inviting feedback from our clients can feel uncomfortable. It may feel tempting to continue on, hoping nobody will criticize us, and that we'll get through the contract and move onto the next one, without anyone giving us any feedback at all—and simply pay us at the end and say goodbye. But how do we learn and grow without feedback, and if we do not know what our clients are thinking or their response to our work, then we are working blindfolded.

Invite feedback as part of the process. Make it easy and open for your clients to tell you what they think, in an objective and constructive way. Practice receiving and giving feedback and not taking it personally. Notice how you feel. If it feels difficult, try to tune in to those feelings. What are they trying to tell you? What might have happened in the past to bring up those feelings, and are they helpful and useful now in this current situation? What can you learn?

Remember that the other person's feedback is likely to be extremely subjective and so finding a way of structuring your feedback process can really help to separate out what is personal from what is going to help you to become a better practitioner.

Reasons why freelancers don't invite feedback:

- We don't want to draw our clients' attention to our failures!
- We went freelance because we dislike the structures of a traditional office environment—including the dreaded annual reviews!
- We are self-critical enough as it is, without someone telling us what we are really bad at!

Feedback can be scary—what if they don't like you, criticize you and it goes deep and stops you moving forward? Or, what if feedback helps you understand what is working well, what is helping you to get new clients and how you can improve and flourish in the future? If you can be brave enough to hold a focus group or conduct some research among your clients and peers, then go for it. If it feels very far outside your comfort zone, then why not take on an independent person to carry out the research for you? Check your clients are happy for their details to be shared and allow someone else to run a survey or series of conversations for you. If budget is an issue, then why not do this for each other—you may be surprised by what you learn. Think very carefully about what you want to know. The questions you feel reluctant to ask may be the ones you need to ask the most! Also, read back any feedback that people have spontaneously shared with you in the past.

Eleanor Goold is a writing coach—in fact she is *my* writing coach—and she says one of the secrets to getting feedback is to send the request as soon as possible after the project has ended:

An effective way to get feedback is via a short customer satisfaction survey.

I currently make good use of a simple Google form that I ask clients to complete at the end of each project. It asks for their feedback on how I can improve as well as the elements about my service that they liked.

It is key to send this as soon as possible after the end of the project while it is still fresh in your client's mind. On the form, I also ask if they would be happy to provide a testimonial. Guided testimonials are often more effective as clients sometimes don't know what to write other than 'Helen was great'. A guided testimonial can help clients write a review that shows how you helped them and the results achieved.

The key is to keep the form concise and easy to complete.

Although it can be challenging, don't view negative feedback as an obstacle or take it personally, instead view it as a perfect opportunity to improve. Client insights on friction points and strategies that you thought were working, but are clearly not, can be a launchpad to not only improve your service but to offer that X factor that will make you stand out from the crowd.

As someone much wiser than me once said 'feedback is the breakfast of champions'.

Security and contingency

So many freelancers simply live in denial of the idea that they may become ill, fall on hard times or even get too busy to service all of their clients. The reality tells a different story. Planning in advance, in a realistic way, about how to manage the unexpected can be reassuring as well as creating a really professional approach—in turn reassuring your clients too.

How to prepare your business in case of illness or unexpected time off (such as bereavement):

- Have an arrangement with another freelancer (or a group of freelancers) who can deputize for you in the event of illness or bereavement or other unexpected situations.
- Work with professionals such as accountants or book-keepers or business advisors and so on, giving you a network to go to if or when you need to ask for help, rather than trying to rush around and find them once you are *in* the emergency.
- Work ahead in the quiet times. Try to prep as much as possible, be your own best friend in this sense and create structures and processes in advance, for everything from admin to content. Try to form an ecosystem that can run itself, such as an online booking system, working with a VA (virtual assistant) and other experts to make your business processes as smooth as possible.

Learning from mistakes

It may be tempting to brush your mistakes under the carpet. There is a certain pressure on freelancers to appear—online and in person—as a perfect swan, swimming merrily through life, living the dream. But of course we make mistakes all the time. We are learning every day, and at the same time, we are also performing the roles of IT manager, CEO, account manager and all those other roles that an agency would offer a client plus we are probably doing this from our own home, which isn't always equipped as well as a slick modern office space. So yes, we make mistakes, just like everyone. The difference is we can choose to have a company culture (even in a company of one!) that celebrates and learns from mistakes. And if we are feeling extremely brave, we can even share what we learned. Obviously in a way that protects our integrity and that of our clients, but learning from and celebrating failure can show a resilience and intelligence that is valuable and sets us apart from our peers.

Trainer and coach Zoe Hawkins explains why we often choose to ignore failure, but why it deserves our attention. She says:

My experience as a coach tells me that a fear of failure gets in the way of people being able to work out what they really want and need.

When I ask my clients "what is it about failure that you're actually afraid of?", many don't know. When I eventually do get answers, I hear things such as:

- Letting people down
- Letting myself down
- Embarrassing myself
- Knowing I could have done better
- Not winning

It seems as though we can be paralyzed from attempting any change just in case it doesn't work out. Even though we know that is how we learn.

Zoe explains why going back to infancy can help us understand that failing is not a bad thing in itself:

Go right back to your roots, watch a baby learn to walk. Watch as they fall down and get back up again. They are not tainted by worrying what other people think of them. They're not concerned with whether or not they'll achieve it. They just apply the same effort to their

50th try as they do their first, learning each time they go and persevering through difficulty, because it's worth it. Failure to them is a First Attempt In Learning (F.A.I.L—see what's been done there?!)

Wouldn't it be great if we could all have the innocence of a baby pursuing their goal?

Reality is, we do worry what people think of us and we are concerned with whether or not we'll achieve, but, being paralyzed through fear is failure. Not trying is failure. Taking the easy option, the safer option, settling for less. It's less than we want for ourselves.

Craig and Aimee, who I talked to about being digital nomads, have found that the *digital* bit can sometimes be the problem . . . they are open about the mistakes and learnings they've made, and how they managed to implement a Plan B. Craig explains:

So, for us, to create the stuff that we create, there's a lot of equipment that goes into it. There are multiple cameras, there's lenses, we've got computers that we carry around with us and there's times where everything goes right and we don't have any problems, all the SD cards work and there's times where an SD card will just corrupt or you won't press record, or sometimes the equipment will fail you, technology will fail you and it's happened to us on a few occasions (multiple times, yeh!). Sometimes it's happened in the middle of huge challenges where we were shooting a series and one of them was—when we did the Mongol Rally—the microphone jack broke on the camera, so we had all this footage that we couldn't use and we had to voice over.

We lost pivotal moments of the whole trip—yeh that was a nightmare—and then—it's happened on paid gigs as well. We went to Germany and did a German castle road and we just—what happened to the SD card? Well it wasn't really technology's fault I believe, I deleted the SD card as I thought we'd backed it up. We deleted it all! That happens as well—so you just have to sort of put up your pictures and look over them and try to bring it back.

Despite losing the footage, the couple used photos and voiceovers to bring the liveliness of the trip to their work. Being incredibly adaptable and agile is so helpful, both when you are working creatively for yourself and when you're traveling.

How to celebrate failure

Books have been written solely on the topic of celebrating failure, and Elizabeth Day's podcast and book *How To Fail* has its own live tour.

Celebrating failure is about celebrating learning, celebrating working outside of our comfort zones and being brave, unafraid to try new things and grow as people and as a business. Like a scientist running a series of experiments or a program of research, we can fail in a measured and thoughtful way—assessing any risks and adapting and learning from what we discover. There can also be a joy to unexpected failures—when I led the marketing team at a craft brewery, the most attention our Instagram feed received was the day when we videoed and shared an overflowing fermentation vessel—the new yeast had caused the beer to explode out of the top of the huge metal vat, with great force. Nobody was hurt, but there was an incredible mess. What it brought to the customers and fans was a sense of authenticity, and a fun look behind the scenes. Part of the culture of craft breweries is that the beer is not mass-produced, there are real people behind each step in the process. Plus it was not set up, and in a world where so much marketing is finely airbrushed and manipulated, that immediacy: "this is happening *now*" also contributed toward the positivity that the brewery's fans share for the brand on social media.

When clients talk to me about failures, I invite them to go through the following process, if they want to, to explore what the learnings might be and look at any changes they might wish to make:

1. Firstly I invited them to state what the failure was—describe what happened and what they felt went wrong.
2. Then we look at the decisions or choices they made which, in retrospect, may have caused the problem.
3. Next we explore what the learnings might be and what they might do differently in future.

4. Then we identify any changes they may wish to make as a result.

5. We look at anything else that may have come up as we discussed this perceived failure, which, on reflection, may not have even been a failure at all.

Clients tend to find this process cathartic as well as practical. Try it yourself and see how you feel. For me, it can help to lay to rest any mistakes that feel like they are hanging over me—it enables me to make a plan to guard against repeating the mistake and equips me for the future.

While reliving the failure may sound painful, I have discovered that when doing this exercise myself and with clients that it can be incredibly cathartic and as well as identifying learnings and opportunities you may not have explored before, there can also be a sense of putting the problem in the past and moving forward, rather than constantly replaying it and feeling bad.

If you feel confident and comfortable enough to share your failure, then you might even choose to use it as material for the contents of a blog post, talk or podcast. Things going wrong is almost always more interesting than a story of perfection! If you do choose to share, then think about how you can do so in a way that keeps you and any other people involved safe in terms of your boundaries and feelings.

Learning from failure: as a photographer

If your talent is capturing once-in-a-lifetime moments, then failure might feel like it isn't an option! Expert event photographer Paul Clarke runs his business in London and has captured significant moments featuring celebrities, royalty and political figures. His insights, as someone who works under pressure regularly, can be applied to a range of creative disciplines. I asked him what he had learned from mistakes, over the years. Paul explains:

There are several layers in which you can think about evaluation and for simplicity, I can describe three of them:

1. **Hard technical:** Are my photos sharp enough? Is my camera choice correct? Am I processing them in an accurate way, so that's the hard-technical stuff.

2. **Soft skills:** Am I managing this client well? Am I reacting well to an increase in scope or an unclear brief? So, all the soft stuff around my business.

3. **Am I doing this right?** This third one, is really easy to miss, and particularly for solo creatives it is the meta one—it sits above all this. It's about 'Am I doing all my business stuff right?', 'Am I working too hard?', 'Am I doing too much stuff?'.

So that's got really nothing to do with the technical aspects of what I do, nor even client management and business building—all of that stuff. It's just knowing 'Have I done enough today?', 'Have I done enough this week?', 'When do I stop?'

And in some ways that third one is the most interesting I think, in terms of practise for creatives. Because you can set measures and goals around it. The first one's the easiest, you can look at other people's work, you can look at reference work, you can look at texts and get some sort of answer on that. Second's a little harder, because it's softer stuff, but again the references and benchmarks are there if you look for them.

The third one is really hard, because why would you do that? It's much easier just to work 150hrs a week than it is to stop and say 'maybe 35 would be ok this week'.

So I evaluate and I do some of those well and some of those not very well at all, which is why I think about them. So that's my first answer: yes let's just pick an area—pick one of those categories and evaluate and analyze.

You get people who obsess about number one for example, and seek every possible form of technical proof that their work is the best—technically it is but maybe they're [still] not doing very well. And that's [perhaps] because they're not doing very well in business: they might not have thought about the soft skills of business building and client management, for example.

Or they might not be doing very well for themselves because they're having a breakdown because they're working incredible hours and have no sense of finished, no sense of done. And in the world we live in for solo creative there isn't a done—you have to set one. I'm very bad at that.

As a coach, I often hear people telling me that they are too busy to spend time evaluating as they are so caught up with the *doing*, and evaluation is like a luxury they can't afford to dedicate time to. But Paul explains that this is a red herring because actually, these tasks can feel very scary and that is what we could focus on here instead of thinking that it's a time issue. So let's explore that a bit more. Why we might be reluctant to evaluate our own work. Because we are scared to!

Paul explains why he used to evade evaluation, and this is likely to ring true for so many independent creative people. He says:

So, the scariest of these for me in terms of the way I do my business is client retention—I know there is a very sensible, rational, evaluative task available to me which is to contact all the clients I haven't heard from in a long time, and ask them why I haven't heard from them in a long time, and ask them what's coming up and keep in touch. It's evaluative because you're asking for reflection and continuity—I do, do it now but it took me years to build a discipline where I do that, and even now I do it in a very limited sense, because it's terrifying!

Clients who hired you three years ago and haven't again, did it for a reason that you don't want to hear. The reason you didn't hear from them was probably because they didn't like a picture, or possibly because they now have someone cheaper.

It's all bad. It's a cascade of bad bad things and in a creative solo business where you and your ego are the product, why would you want to listen to a whole afternoon of people telling you why they stopped working with you? And yet it's incredibly good evaluation. I think it took me eight years of the business before I even dared do anything [like this], eight years before I ever contacted a client proactively. I didn't have a problem because I had lots of work, I'm quite sensible about these things.

So [now], I do a monthly review. I set a time window, so if it's March I look at June. So, every March I look at what happened in June in the last three years, because a lot of my work is cyclical, and it's also just a good disciplined way—one year isn't always helpful but three years is good.

I look in my calendar and note what was I doing on June 19, 18 and 17 and all of those clients who I have not heard from—and that kind of gives me my shopping list. And then I say to them: "You held the 34th 35th and 36th annual awards for your industry in those years— I'm guessing the 37th will be happening this year—shall we book it?" So it's a good systematic way—but it does mean you are contacting people who are going to say 'oh actually we're not coming back to you, not using you anymore, wanted a change', and whatever reason they give, it usually hurts a bit.

Because my product is artistic and creative, I can't guarantee I'm going to satisfy every client in every possible way. I can't guarantee that. There's a lot of truth in the phrase, 'people don't remember what you said or what you did, they just remember how you made them feel.' I live a lot by this phrase, unfortunately the problem with photos is that they very often make you feel something.

I reflected with Paul about how our creative work can often take a shortcut right into people's psychology. And what starts out as a transaction between two businesses becomes about their feelings, and then can have a knock-on effect and become about the creative's feelings too. So you have two people entering into a business deal, but it turns out to be a transaction about our feelings of inadequacy perhaps, which is totally different from commissioning some headshots for a corporate website for example. Another example we discussed was a PR shoot, and if the result is a set of photos that did not get picked up by the press for some reason, then the PR might not wish to work with that photographer again, but there are so many other factors that might affect that outcome.

We noticed that when you're evaluating your work and learning, then the learnings have got to take into account the context and what's going on—the story and what's going on behind that, the circumstances, what the brief was and what's going on for that person. It's not a binary process when evaluating it, not simply asking: "Was it a good job or a bad job?" And this isn't about letting ourselves off the hook where we know we could improve but equally we cannot take on board those factors that are out of our control either.

Implementing plan B (or C or D)

If what your evaluation tells you is you're not hitting your financial targets from your current work, and you've been implementing *Plan A* for some time, well you might want or need to take a different route from where you are now to reach your destination. Pivoting, having a *side-hustle*, not keeping all your eggs in one basket . . . whatever you call it. For me, as I come from a financial PR background, it is diversification, as in not investing everything in the same place.

I talked about this with Alexis Hightower, who is a talented artist, musician, singer and performer in New York, about the difference between goals and reality and how we can combat this as creative freelancers. She's opened for the likes of Gil Scott-Heron and Bobby McFerrin and yet, despite reaching these heights, she's completely realistic about the need to diversify:

> *Creative freelancers need three things in my opinion: flexibility, energy and a deeply rooted belief in themselves. I say flexibility first because it's very rare that things go exactly as planned. Your goal might be to star on Broadway. On your way to that goal you may need to teach voice, perform audiobooks, sing on songwriter demos, perform in off-off-off Broadway workshops, reinvent yourself as a music producer, dog walk, develop a skin care line, babysit. You get the idea. So, you have to be flexible about your goals and be willing to diversify. And let's be honest. All the biggest stars diversify as a function of status. There's a reason that Rihanna has a clothing and makeup brand, Jay-Z owns a streaming service. Kelly Clarkson has a morning show. Diversifying and being flexible is the name of the game. It takes energy because the*

creative freelance life is a long slog and you need to stay focused and continually invest in improving your skill set. People who are successful pursue their goals with a kind of tireless zeal. It takes energy and focus to do that. And then, self-belief as I described before. It's sometimes the only thing that will get you through the bad times.

Combating the *Sunday night fear*

If you're stuck in a contract you hate or things feel like an uphill struggle right now, then the fear of Monday mornings can sometimes begin on a Sunday night . . . I've drawn up some ways to help you combat that so-called *Sunday Night Fear*, in addition to using this book to help you plan your way to a better contract or to a more fulfilling future.

- *Write down what it is that you don't want to face.* What the actions—or possible actions—are and whether you have any other options. Consider who could help or support you with these tasks and what else you could do. Think about how you might reward yourself once you've completed the work.
- *Recall what you do that makes you feel better when you are up against it and what might help you now.* Whether it's a hot bath, country walk or having a good moan to a friend over a little glass of wine… work out what you could do to help you regroup and feel ready to tackle whatever Monday morning might bring—a good night's sleep is often going to help, which goes without saying!
- *Create a Sunday night routine.* And stick to it. If you know that a bath, clean bed linen and an early night with a good book can help you create a conducive environment to refreshing sleep and a productive Monday morning, then try to avoid getting in your own way—block out that time in your diary and keep it for you.
- *Turning your fear into excitement.* This may sound impossible, but if you think about the symptoms of fear and the

symptoms of feeling excited, then there is not a huge amount of difference. Imagine a first date with someone you are really attracted to, then think about a meeting you don't really want to go to. A lot of the feelings of anxiety will be similar. Imagine that fear as excitement—motivated by the desire to do a great job, adrenaline caused by excitement instead of by fear. What does it feel like, this excitement? What can you do to help yourself to feel calm instead of excited (or scared)? Think about your routine—one client admitted to me that their tendency to drink three cups of strong coffee before giving a presentation really doesn't help them to feel calm (no surprises there!), so a simple action such as packing a few sachets of calming chamomile tea in your bag on the way to a big meeting or conference might ensure that caffeine isn't the only option when you arrive. Think about how you would keep a colleague or client calm if they were anxious about something. Are there any elements of that which you can do for yourself? Your own advice is good, you know you best and sometimes it's just a case of reminding yourself that going for a walk or getting an early night can make the difference between meltdown and mastering your day.

How to stay current

Staying current and connected can support and nurture your creativity and help you to generate the best creative ideas for clients. These opportunities might contribute to improved wellbeing too. Ways to stay current will look different for everyone and might include:

- Being part of festivals and awards, whether as a guest, judge, speaker or exhibitor.
- Working from stimulating locations—a trip to an art gallery, hot-desking at a friend's creative studio.
- Volunteering for a charity—using your skills or learning new ones.

- Attending talks, tours and lectures.
- Asking a friend or contact to show you around their workplace and tell you about how they do things—I love meeting pals who work at interesting digital businesses, and getting a sense for their environment. I've encountered rooftop running tracks and meeting rooms named after rock stars as well as some of the most adorable office dogs on my journeys.
- Collaborating with another freelancer you respect on a project.
- A daytime cinema trip.
- A tour of a food or drink (or other interesting) factory—from chocolate to gin and cheese to beer, I've always learned something new and inspiring from doing these myself.
- The way so many of us creative founders and freelancers work today—communicating daily via e-mail and video calls, or via social networks—is incredibly new. What we may take for granted, such as online banking apps or Wi-Fi calling for example, simply did not exist for those of us freelancing just a few decades back and in fact would have felt like science fiction to me in my school days.

We can learn a lot from those who worked for themselves in creative roles when I was growing up in the 1980s and early 1990s: the resourcefulness and tenacity required back then can be applied today by those of us who want not just to survive but to thrive.

When my friend Nancy Durham worked as a journalist in the 1980s, she often used telephone booths to communicate with her clients when she was out and about. This was not at all unusual at that time. In fact, it was how I'd communicate with my parents if I wanted to be picked up from a party, for example. What has not changed since that time is how competitive journalism was and still is today. To excel, you need to have the spark that Nancy had, and like Nancy did, discover your niche or unique selling point:

I was a fully employed news and current affairs reporter with CBC Radio in Canada when I decided to emigrate to the UK. This was in 1984 and I arrived in March of that year. CBC had a large vibrant bureau in London so I headed straight for it to see how I might fit in. It was not easy. There was a fierce pecking order and I found myself at the bottom of the ladder. Other freelancers— British, American, Canadian—hung out there and generously shared information about their "strings". Stringer was often used as another word for freelancer back then. From them I learned of opportunities at National Public Radio in the U.S., Deutsche Welle's English broadcast service in Germany and outlets in Ireland and all around London.

Never mind the superfast wifi we take for granted today, there wasn't even email. Telephone calls were all via landlines and so I used telephone booths. No one had a mobile phone. I'd ring an editor or an editor's assistant and actually talk to someone and arrange a meeting, face-to-face, in a newspaper lobby or radio station. Looking back it seems extraordinary that one could actually get to see important people just by ringing and asking.

Nancy developed her specialism by noticing a niche and stepping into it—a tip that still holds true for creative freelancers today. One of the biggest mistakes I see founders and freelancers making every day is to wait to see what work comes in, then competing for those briefs instead of being proactive. Those people who are making great careers for themselves are thinking ahead, seeing the opportunities, networking and noticing where they can add value. Nancy identified countries she could be relied on to go to, and topics she could really own, reporting from where the stories were unfolding in front of her eyes:

Freelancers get to go where they want to go and this allows them to develop specialties few others have. I went regularly to Czechoslovakia in the eighties and by the time the Velvet Revolution came along in 1989 I was known as someone to go to for stories there. I was on the scene in the days leading up to the fall of the communists and stayed for weeks reporting daily, sometimes hourly, and ended up with a full time reporting job with the CBC. That ended my freelance career for some years.

To me, sitting at my desk in sunny Hay-on-Wye in Wales, it sounds like Nancy was incredibly brave too. To her, it was about seeing the opportunity, having a nose for news and owning her career. From my safe rural space, it sounds slightly terrifying! Nancy's golden piece of advice for current or aspiring freelance reporters looking to build a sustainable career is:

Go somewhere that's under reported, make it yours and tell the world what you find.

These days Nancy runs FARMERS' Welsh Lavender—in fact she founded the first lavender farm in Wales—where she creates unique and sustainable products with her team at their beautiful and tranquil headquarters. Once again she noticed a niche and stepped into it. And you can do the same if you can bring tenacity and passion to your work every day.

Conclusion

Over two years of researching this book, I learned that thriving means completely different things to different people. On this journey, I've immersed myself in so many different versions of thriving and experienced the joy of all of them through briefly stepping into the shoes of each founder.

I was reluctant to take on board, like many of us who believe themselves to be inherently creative, the emphasis around creating structure and systems and adopting routines and habits. I started this journey with very few good habits and several bad ones. I'd come to associate structure with a form of restriction, and it was my idea of giving in, or giving up.

In fact, the opposite is true. I've learned that creating good habits, and healthy structures and systems, actually frees us up to fulfill our creative potential rather than holding us back.

I've also discovered the energy and inspiration I get from listening to others' learnings: the wins and the fails both teach me about the power and resilience of those of us who feel inspired enough to go it alone. And I've also discovered that a life, which I once saw as lonely—that of freelancer or founder—can be the most profoundly connected and supported. I can count on one hand the amount of people who refused my interview requests, and yet the amount of support and offers of help and ideas I've received has been overwhelming.

If you truly want to thrive as an independent creative—and remember you do have to want it—then take just the tips and ideas that feel relevant to you and go out there and enjoy the journey. Enjoy not only the wins, but also the ditches and potholes, in fact, especially those. Please let me know how you get on; I'd love to hear about *your* journey and I'd like to keep on sharing the stories that can teach all of us about how to be the best and happiest creatives we can be.

References

Articles and studies

Freelancing in America 2019 survey: Upwork
The State of Remote Work report: Buffer
Capital Group Survey 2018
MarketInvoice Business Insights research 2019 (Now MarketFinance)
Research on the financial welfare of the self-employed: IPSE
Working for Yourself 2018: IPA
PayPal Global Freelancer Insights Report 2018

Recommended reading

- Big Magic by Elizabeth Gilbert
- The Artist's Way by Julia Cameron
- Time to Think by Nancy Kline
- Better Than Before by Gretchen Rubin

About the author

Helen works as a life and business coach for ambitious and creative entrepreneurs.

Clients seek her help to bring more joy, energy and abundance into their lives, to create space and reconnect with their self-worth and creative freedom.

Prior to becoming a coach, Helen spent two decades of her career in PR and comms strategy, with a focus on building and leading effective teams and working directly with decision-makers and CEOs.

She lives in the famous book town of Hay-on-Wye on the Welsh border and enjoys working with artistic clients around the world, bringing her authenticity and energy to all she does. As well as writing and coaching, she also enjoys being in nature, festivals, food, music and art.

Index

OTHER TITLES IN THE ENTREPRENEURSHIP AND SMALL BUSINESS MANAGEMENT COLLECTION

Scott Shane, Case Western University, Editor

- *Blockchain Value* by Olga V. Mack
- *TAP Into Your Potential* by Rick De La Guardia
- *Stop, Change, Grow* by Michael Carter and Karl Shaikh
- *A Cynicâ's Business Wisdom* by Jay J. Silverberg
- *Dynastic Planning* by Walid S. Chiniara
- *From Starting Small to Winning Big* by Shishir Mishra
- *How to Succeed as a Solo Consultant* by Stephen D. Field
- *Small Business Management* by Andreas Karaoulanis
- *Native American Entrepreneurs* by Ron P. Sheffield and Mark J. Munoz
- *The Entrepreneurial Adventure* by David James and Oliver James
- *On All Cylinders, Second Edition* by Ron Robinson
- *Cultivating an Entrepreneurial Mindset* by Tamiko L. Cuellar
- *From Vision to Decision* by Dana K. Dwyer
- *Get on Board* by Olga V. Mack
- *The Rainmaker* by Jacques Magliolo
- *Department of Startup* by Ivan Yong Wei Kit and Sam Lee
- *Family Business Governance* by Keanon J. Alderson

Concise and Applied Business Books

The Collection listed above is one of 30 business subject collections that Business Expert Press has grown to make BEP a premiere publisher of print and digital books. Our concise and applied books are for...

- Professionals and Practitioners
- Faculty who adopt our books for courses
- Librarians who know that BEP's Digital Libraries are a unique way to offer students ebooks to download, not restricted with any digital rights management
- Executive Training Course Leaders
- Business Seminar Organizers

Business Expert Press books are for anyone who needs to dig deeper on business ideas, goals, and solutions to everyday problems. Whether one print book, one ebook, or buying a digital library of 110 ebooks, we remain the affordable and smart way to be business smart. For more information, please visit www.businessexpertpress.com, or contact sales@businessexpertpress.com.

Lightning Source UK Ltd.
Milton Keynes UK
UKHW022216150421
382056UK00006B/209